Design your own knits in 5 easy steps

Design your own knits
in 5 easy steps

Debbie Abrahams

hamlyn

An Hachette Livre UK company

First published in Great Britain in 2008 by Hamlyn,
a division of Octopus Publishing Group Ltd
2–4 Heron Quays, London E14 4JP
www.octopusbooks.co.uk

Distributed in the United States and Canada
by Sterling Publishing Co., Inc.
387 Park Avenue South,
New York, NY 10016-8810

ISBN: 978-0-600-61638-2

A CIP catalogue record for this book is available
from the British Library

Printed and bound in China

10 9 8 7 6 5 4 3 2 1

CONTENTS

Introduction

Hand-knitting is a fascinating craft through which a multitude of projects can be created. The unique stretch of knitting makes it a versatile fabric that works wonderfully well for both garments and accessories. And, because you are in control of making the fabric, you can choose whatever colour you like, work with your favourite fibre and fashion it to specific measurements, resulting in a project that is truly tailor-made.

This book guides you through the whole creative process of designing your own knits in five easy steps, from conception to the finished project. And it really is quite simple. Step 1 focuses on the starting point of your design – your inspiration – and shows you how you can use it to generate ideas for colour, texture and pattern. Step 2 guides you through the process of transferring your ideas onto graph paper so that they can be knitted and Step 3 gives you advice on knitting up that all-important swatch. Step 4 gets down to the nitty-gritty of how to calculate the stitches and rows for your design. And finally, Step 5 offers tips on calculating the amount of yarn needed for different projects and how to write up your pattern so you are ready to start knitting. It also includes advice on constructing basic shapes for garments and accessories, including bags, sweaters, socks and skirts. Easy, isn't it!

Your knitting can be developed into something really special by adding embellishments like beads, buttons, sequins and embroidery, or you can experiment with the stitches themselves to create unique effects like cables and lacework. If you like using colour you can easily transform a regular piece of knitting into a stunning fabric, especially if embellishments, textured stitches and colours are all combined together. The possibilities are endless!

So, if you've ever had a desire to design your own knits, there is nothing stopping you from picking up your needles and having a go. All you need is your imagination, motivation and a love of the craft, and with this book you can embark on a wonderful creative journey that will turn your ideas into fabulous pieces of knitting.

STEP 1 INSPIRATION, STITCHES AND YARN

Finding inspiration

Inspiration is a very personal thing and you need to create a strong design idea before starting work on any knitting project.

Look for inspiration everywhere and anywhere; consider other knitted items – perhaps from your childhood – or the colours in a favourite china tea set. Your inspiration will be the main focus for your knitted design and it will help generate ideas for colour, texture and patterning (see pages 13–25). So it must be something that is really special, that evokes a passionate response in you and feeds your imagination with creative thoughts.

Sources of inspiration are usually either the natural world around us or man-made products. Autumn leaves can provide a vibrant palette of sumptuous colours for a design, just as geometric motifs on a roll of wallpaper can spark off ideas for a bold, graphic pattern. However, sometimes your inspiration can come from a less obvious source – the colours you see in the sky at sunset, or a glimpse of a gorgeous garden from the bus window on the way home from work.

A pile of autumn leaves in vibrant shades of red, orange and yellow can provide a wealth of inspiration for a design.

With so many visual references surrounding us in our everyday lives, there is an infinite library of inspiration always at our disposal. To create wonderful, unique designs you must try to develop your own creative senses by being receptive to everything you see around you. Take time to absorb and appreciate the colours, shapes and patterns in whatever you are looking at.

What inspires you?

So first of all, before you even think about picking up those knitting needles, you need to ask yourself what inspires *you*. Sometimes there is an easier answer to this question than you might think. Are you a collector of anything? It could be that you collect colourful glass vases, ceramic pots, hand-painted tiles, old photographs, foreign stamps or paintings, all of which would make a wonderful starting point for your design.

Alternatively, if you are a keen gardener or someone who enjoys the outdoor life, so you might find inspiration in the huge variety of flora and fauna that surrounds you every day.

Remember that what you are looking for is a starting point for your design and it really can be anything you like. So if you find something that inspires you, just go for it and let your creative juices flow.

Picture perfect

Look through old photograph albums to see if anything catches your eye. Maybe you have interesting snapshots of objects, people or places that you have long forgotten about.

Or what about that pile of magazines that you've hoarded away for years in the loft? A quick flick through them might be just what you need to find a great visual reference for a design.

Creating a mood board

It is a good idea to build up a personal library of images by collecting together any visual material that you come across and admire. For example, your inspiration might come from African jewellery, so you will collect as many relevant interesting pictures as you can.

Photographs, postcards and cuttings from magazines can all be pasted down onto a board to create an exciting and stimulating focal point for your ideas. Designers refer to this as a 'mood board'. Creating your own mood board can really help to get your ideas flowing and, like drawing and sketching, will focus your attention on elements of your inspiration that might not have been obvious to you when you first looked at the pictures.

Recognizing inspiration

We are surrounded by different colours, patterns and shapes in the natural world around us, as well as in man-made products. Even the most common things have huge design potential.

During a casual walk in the countryside you will no doubt come across a wealth of visual stimulation: the rigid vertical structure of an old wooden fence, the golden shimmer of a ripe wheat field, the random patterning on an ancient tree stump, or the subtle tones of lichens and mosses on a weathered stone wall. Here, before your eyes, are patterns and shapes and colours that already exist in nature – they are just waiting for you to notice them. The process of sketching these inspirational things will help you to see them more clearly. In fact, this is the first step in breaking down what you see into separate elements.

Making sketches

To create your own design, first look carefully at your source of inspiration and decide which elements you want to focus on. Making sketches and homing in on the colours, patterns and textures that you see will help you to identify the key elements that will form the basis of your design.

You don't have to be a master of art to make sketches. You just need to have some good art materials to work with that you feel comfortable using: paints, coloured pencils, chalks, pastels, inks, charcoal or collage are just a few of the options you can choose from.

Choosing art materials

Your choice of art materials will be influenced by your subject matter and how you want to interpret it. For example, gouache paints are great for flat areas of colour because they cover the surface area well and are opaque, so you might opt to use these if your design consists of precise shapes, such as geometric or striped patterns in bright blocks of colour.

Alternatively, chalks and pastels can be smudged together to give subtle colour changes, so these might suit you better if your inspiration comes from something more organic and less rigid, such as the soft colours in a landscape that blend to give a mixture of shades.

Be prepared

Keep a camera in your bag at all times so that when you see something inspirational you can capture it on film. You might come across an unexpected visual treat even during a boring trip to the supermarket, so don't forget to carry your camera.

Soft pastels in shades of violet, green and yellow are gently blended together to create this drawing of a serene and peaceful landscape.

Drawing for yourself

It is important to remember that your interpretation of the subject and how you choose to draw it may differ from everyone else's interpretation of it. But this doesn't matter – in fact this is what makes each new design individual.

Don't worry about how good or bad your drawing and painting skills may be. Your sketches are for your personal use and not for anyone else's eyes. This preliminary sketching is just a tool to enable you to realize your ideas in the form of knitting.

Developing sketches

You might have to make more sketches to develop your ideas further, although this will depend on what you want your final design to be. If it is going to be a very literal interpretation of your inspiration, such as a face or an animal, then you might consider making a tracing of your drawing and transferring that straight onto proportional graph paper (see page 32), which you will find at the back of this book.

If you want to develop your design into a more abstract motif or a repeat pattern, then you may need to do more work on your existing drawings. For example, you can experiment with duplicating a shape several times and rotating it to see what happens. This can result in a great design for an all-over pattern repeat, or it might look effective as an edging pattern.

Seeing colours and shapes

This isn't always as easy as it sounds; it's quite a skill to see all the different colours in everyday things. If you study the shadows created by changes in light, you may think at first glance that the colours you see in them are all shades of grey. However, after a closer look you may conclude that in fact the shadows are made up from various shades of blue, purple and violet, as in this painting.

In the same way, shapes will become obvious when you start sketching. Let's say that you have chosen a photograph of a landscape for your inspiration. At first you may see only very irregular shapes, such as trees, bushes and fields that appear to have no connection to each other. But on a second look those bushes could be seen as ovals and circles and the fields as horizontal bands of colour. You can then refine your drawing, reducing it down to basic structures and essentials. This may mean not including every single line or splash of colour that you see, but being more selective and picking out the most important elements.

You need to constantly remind yourself that these ideas are going to be developed into a knitted design, and it will be impossible to include every single detail.

Dots of colour in blue, purple and violet are combined to create the impression of shadows on the ground of a woodland.

Understanding colour

Choosing what colours you are going to use can be one of the most important decisions that you have to make about your design, and for some people it can also be one of the hardest.

Many people claim that they have no sense of colour and struggle to decide which colours will work well together. However, don't ever tell yourself this because everyone has a sense of colour, it's just that some people have developed it more than others. If you are open-minded and allow your senses to soak up the colour combinations around you, then you will gradually build up your own colour sense.

Cool and warm colours

The colours that you choose for your design will inevitably evoke some sort of mood or emotion, because this is what colours do. Put simply, there are cool colours and warm colours and your design might focus on either one of these colour palettes, or possibly combine the two to provide contrasts.

A cool palette includes shades of green, blue and violet and these are often interpreted as quiet, soothing colours. A warm colour palette includes shades of magenta, crimson, red, orange and yellow and can be interpreted as spicy, fiery colours that evoke more passionate emotions.

Colour symbolism

Some colours are also symbolic when used in a particular context and this context differs around the world. For example, in the West red signals danger while in many Eastern countries it signifies luck.

Colour theory

Colours can be broken down into different categories. These are:

Primary colours Red, yellow and blue.

Secondary colours Orange, green and purple. These are created by mixing two primary colours. (Blue mixed with yellow creates green, blue mixed with red creates purple and red mixed with yellow creates orange.)

Tertiary colours These are created by mixing a primary colour with the closest secondary colour to give a variation of a secondary colour and so extend the colour palette. (For example, primary yellow mixed with secondary green makes tertiary light apple-green.)

Complementary colours These colours have the least in common and are on opposite sides of the colour wheel. (For example, orange is the complementary of blue and red is the complementary of green.)

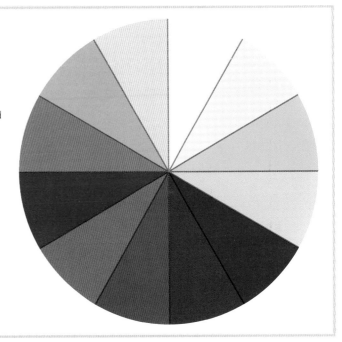

Generally, green has associations with the outdoors, nature and health and blue suggests calm, restfulness and quiet. So you need to think carefully about the colours that you choose and the associations that they have, as this can have a big impact on your design and on the mood that it creates.

Using colours

Using just primary colours will create a bright and simple effect, often seen in children's toys where immediate appeal is essential. If secondary colours are introduced the palette is extended and becomes more subtle. Tertiary colours further extend the palette into an enormous range of tints and shades.

For dramatic effect you can use complementary colours in your design to really spice it up. A green background colour with splashes of red on it will look almost three-dimensional. Alternatively, you can deliberately restrict yourself to a limited palette and so create more subtle effects. You might choose to use a range of just grey and blue shades, which will create a very cool and placid effect.

Combining colours

Any colour is affected by other colours around it and so, depending on what is next to it, a red may look bluer or a green yellower. You can explore this by knitting basic two-colour stripe patterns (see pages 23 and 42–43) in different colour combinations to see how the colours respond to each other.

What you need to achieve in your design is a combination of colours that are harmonious and relate to each other in a pleasing way. Successful designs are about getting the colour combinations just right. So you need to ask yourself what mood do you want your design to create; how do you want it to make you feel? The subject matter and colours of your inspiration will already have provided you with some of the answers to these questions, but you are in control of your colour palette and you should always remember that you can change your mind about it at any time if you feel that it is not working.

Colour vision

Do you know that a colour appears darker when the colour around it is lighter, and that the same colour appears lighter when the colour around it is darker? You can test this by painting the same coloured shape onto two different background colours.

Creating your colour palette

Your colour palette should come from your inspiration and the subsequent drawings or sketches you made from it. You probably chose your inspiration not only because of its subject matter, but because you were attracted to the colours in it – even if this was a subconscious decision.

Your inspiration will also guide you as to how much emphasis you need to give to each individual colour in your design. You will probably need to look at your drawings again to see this more clearly. Look at which colours dominate and then pick out the ones to use as highlights. For your design to be successful you really need to imitate the original colour balance as closely as possible.

It is best to start off with several colours in your palette and then you can narrow it down to a select few as you progress further through the design process. As long as you don't stray too far from your original inspiration it is perfectly all right to tweak the colours in your palette if you think that this will result in a more pleasing design.

In fact, you will probably find that when you look at the available yarns you will have to compromise on some of the colours you originally selected. Although good yarn stores have a great selection of colours to choose from, it is likely that the exact shade of blue you picked out as a key colour cannot be perfectly matched. So you will have to compromise and go for the nearest shade available.

Yarns come in a limited palette of shades that might not match all the colours in your inspiration, so you might have to compromise on your selection.

From inspiration to knitting

The next step is to interpret what you have sketched on paper into something knitted. Depending on how complex you want your design to be, you can experiment with just one of these techniques or combine several of them to create more spectacular effects (see page 25).

Textured stitches

Stocking/stockinette stitch is created by knitting every stitch on right-side rows and by purling every stitch on wrong-side rows. Doing the opposite creates reverse stocking/stockinette stitch. You can knit a stocking/stockinette stitch background fabric with textured patterns in purl stitches, or a reverse stocking/stockinette stitch background fabric with textured patterns in knit stitches. Motifs and repeat patterns look effective knitted either way around.

Garter stitch

If you knit every stitch on both right-side and wrong-side rows you will create garter stitch. This stitch looks like a series of horizontal waves and can be effective if it is knitted in blocks within a stocking/stockinette stitch fabric. You will need to knit more rows in garter stitch than in stocking/stockinette stitch to make both fabrics the same length because garter stitch condenses the rows. Garter stitch is used a lot for edgings on garments because it creates a firm fabric that does not pull in or stretch (see page 39).

Garter stitch is one of the easiest textured stitches to knit and creates regular, horizontal waves across the knitting.

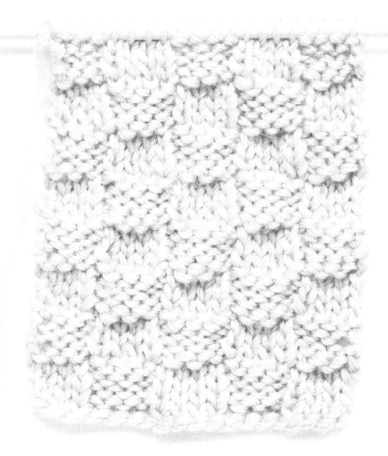

Basketweave creates a strong geometric pattern of rectangular blocks in knit and purl stitches that can be easily varied in size, depending on your design.

Moss/seed stitch

This is created on rows with an odd number of stitches by knitting one stitch and then purling one stitch and repeating this across all rows. For rows with an even number of stitches this is created by knitting one stitch and then purling one stitch and then on the next row purling one stitch and then knitting one stitch, and so on. In comparison to stocking/stockinette stitch, moss/seed stitch will spread out the width of stitches and condense the rows, so sometimes it is better to knit it on a needle one size smaller.

Moss/seed stitch-stripes and geometric shapes, or just simply an all-over pattern repeat, can look great in a one-colour design. This stitch is also often used as an edging for garments because it creates a firm fabric (see page 39).

Basketweave stitch

This stitch looks like a raised checkerboard and can be knitted in a variety of different ways to achieve different-size basketweave patterns. The sample shown here is based on a combination of knitting four stitches, then purling four stitches. The number of stitches and rows in the pattern repeat will dictate how big or small the basketweave is.

This is a great stitch for simulating the regular patterns that you might see in a brick wall or a tiled roof because it creates a strong tessellated pattern. It can be used in selected areas or as an all-over repeat design.

A slip-stitch pattern with the yarn held to the front of the work will create small bars across the knitting which gives it a honeycomb look.

Ribs

These are vertical, textured patterns that can be knitted in a variety of different stitches. Ribs are typically stretchy fabrics that open up and recover back and so they are used a lot for edgings on garments (see page 39).

Single (1 x 1) rib is created by knitting one stitch and purling one stitch and repeating this across all right-side rows. On all wrong-side rows the pattern is reversed so that the stitches that were knitted are purled, and the stitches that were purled are knitted.

Double (2 x 2) rib is created in a similar way, but two stitches are knitted and then purled instead of one. You could also try combining ribs with moss/seed stitch to create a more textured look.

Rib stitches are perfect for interpreting all sorts of vertical patterns that you might see in your inspiration, for example a slatted fence or the columns in an ancient Greek ruin.

Slip-stitch patterns

These are achieved by slipping selected stitches across a right-side row instead of knitting or purling them. On wrong-side rows the slipped stitches are usually worked in purl. This looks really effective in a ribbed fabric because it makes the slipped stitches appear more prominent.

When you slip the stitches you can hold the yarn at either the front or the back of the work and this will create very different effects. Held at the front, the yarn will leave a bar across the stitch. Held at the back, the stitch will be slightly elongated and will look embossed. Slip-stitch fabrics are usually tighter and less elastic than stocking/stockinette stitch.

Bobbles

Bobbles are created by working several times into one stitch to create extra stitches, and then working back and forth across these stitches a number of times to create extra fabric. The extra stitches are then decreased, resulting in a bobble.

You can alter the size of a bobble by working as many times as you want into the one stitch, or by working back and forth across the stitches as many times as you want – the more times, the bigger the bobble. Bobbles are usually knitted in stocking/stockinette stitch, but there is nothing stopping you from experimenting with textured bobbles created by working the stitches in moss or garter stitch.

Bobbles look great in all-over repeat patterns, in Aran patterns (where they are traditionally used), or they can be used in a slightly more humorous way to knit noses or eyes for animals or faces.

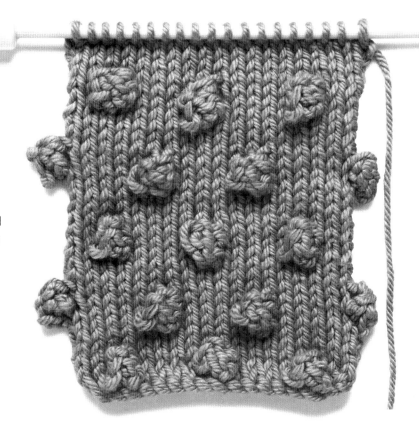

Textured bobbles on a background of stocking/stockinette stitch create a tactile and fun fabric. They also look great combined with cables, as in traditional Aran patterns.

Cables

There are many different patterns that can be created by cabling stitches, but they are all based on the same technique. Sets of stitches are crossed over each other at regular intervals to give the fabric an embossed look. The stitches that are cabled are usually knitted in stocking/stockinette stitch with the stitches between the cables knitted in reverse stocking/stockinette stitch, and this is what makes them look embossed.

When the stitches are crossed over each other they can be held at either the front or the back of the work. If they are held at the front, the cable will twist to the left and if the stitches are held at the back, the cable will twist to the right. The number of stitches in a cable can be any number you choose, with any number of rows worked between them and this is what dictates the size of a cable – the more stitches and rows in a cable, the bigger the cable will knit up.

Cabled stitches pull the width of the knitting in so you usually have to either increase stitches to accommodate a cable or cast on more stitches to achieve the correct width fabric (see pages 40–41).

Cables are traditionally used in Aran patterns with other stitches such as bobbles (see above), but their fluidity could be used to simulate organic sources of inspiration such as plants, the natural patterns you might see in wood grain or the entangled roots of an aged tree.

Lace

This is a very open-looking fabric that is made up from a series of eyelets and stitches in a repeat pattern. Stitches are decreased in a row and then increased again, so that across a pattern repeat the number of stitches is maintained (see also page 41).

There are several different ways that the stitches can be increased and they depend on whether the stitches before and after the increase are knit or purl. There are also several different ways that the stitches can be decreased and they will alter the way the lace stitches look, creating a smoother or more textured fabric. The stitches between the eyelets can be worked in either knit or purl to create further variations in the pattern.

Lace fabrics are usually quite light and airy and consequently they work well in finer-weight yarns. Lace can be knitted in selected areas or as panels in a piece of knitting, or it can be used as an all-over repeat pattern.

Lace patterns are created by decreasing and then increasing stitches within a pattern repeat. This results in a light, open fabric that has an elegant and delicate quality.

Multi-coloured patterns

Different coloured yarns can be used in one piece of knitting to create multi-coloured patterns. Tiny repeat patterns, logos, letters and all sorts of motifs can be knitted into a design quite easily. There are two different techniques that are used to produce coloured patterns in hand-knitting and they are used for two very different types of design.

Intarsia

This is one of two ways to create multi-coloured knitted fabric. Any designs that involve blocks or areas of colour will be knitted using the intarsia technique. It produces a single-thickness fabric that has no yarns carried across the back of the work. Instead, individual balls of yarn are joined into the work when they are needed to knit a block of colour. The yarns can be wound onto bobbins to help keep them separate or they can be cut into long lengths.

The most important thing to remember about this technique is that the yarns have to be crossed at the back of the work on every row to stop holes from appearing between the colour changes.

A lot of geometric and tessellated patterns work well using the intarsia technique (see also page 42), as do individual motifs such as pictures or letters. The flat, even fabric of a piece of intarsia knitting should match the tension/gauge of stocking/stockinette stitch.

Here is a simple chart for an individual motif (in this case, a duck). Only one contrasting colour is used, represented in the chart using colour rather than a symbol.

This motif of a duck has been knitted using the intarsia technique. The green yarn for the background colour was divided into separate balls to work around the yellow duck.

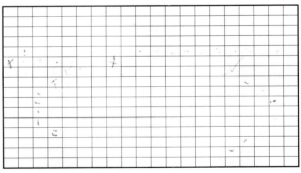

The chart for the duck motif shows more clearly the different blocks of colour that need to be identified and then knitted using separate balls of yarn.

Fair Isle

This is best described as a multi-coloured, busy repeat pattern knitted in stocking/stockinette stitch. Traditional Fair Isle patterns use only two colours in each row, but the whole design can use as many colours as you want.

A double-thickness fabric is created by stranding or floating the yarn that is not being used across the back of the work. Long strands across more than three stitches can be woven into the back of the work to keep it neat and tidy. A Fair Isle fabric will be tighter in tension/gauge than stocking/stockinette stitch, so sometimes it is wise to use a needle one size larger to knit it.

Fair Isle patterns create very warm fabrics and work well knitted in something like a 4-ply or double-knitting-weight yarn. These yarns will produce a very desirable fabric that is not too heavy, despite it being double thickness.

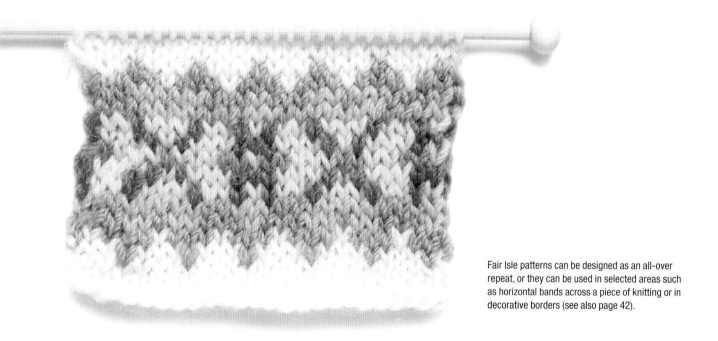

Fair Isle patterns can be designed as an all-over repeat, or they can be used in selected areas such as horizontal bands across a piece of knitting or in decorative borders (see also page 42).

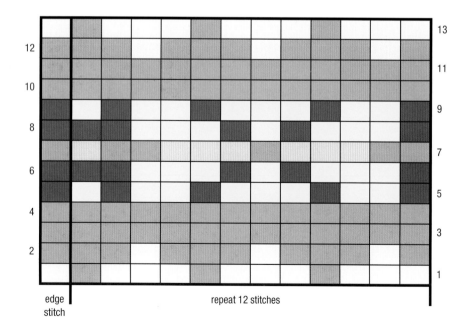

edge stitch

repeat 12 stitches

Stripes

These are great fun because you can very easily create a really colourful design that is simple to knit and you can combine whatever colours you like to give all sorts of effects. If you choose a range of colours in similar shades you will get a stripe pattern that has subtle shading. But if you choose two contrasting colours, such as black and white, this will create a much stronger effect that will be dazzling to the eye. It is also worth noting that when two contrasting colours are used in a stripe, the darker stripes will look narrower than the lighter ones – this is simply an optical illusion (see page 14).

You can experiment with the width of stripes in a pattern and make them regular or varied, depending on the look you want to achieve. Or why not introduce a bit of texture to give your stripes a different look (see chevron stripes below)?

Your inspiration might be a deckchair that has a regular stripe pattern, or it might be something less precise, such as the changing colours in a landscape that you want to interpret as subtle stripes to capture the mood and feel of what you are seeing.

Chevron stripes are created by working this chevron stitch pattern and changing colour as for ordinary horizontal stripes.

Embellishments

Plain knitted fabrics can be transformed into something really special by embellishing. Features on garments, like collars, pockets or edgings can be highlighted, and accessories can also look stunning with a little embellishment.

Beads

These are easily knitted into a fabric to create sparkling, eye-catching effects. The beads are threaded onto the yarn before casting on, so it is crucial that the hole through the middle of them is large enough for the yarn to pass through. There are several different ways to knit in beads, but one of the most popular techniques is to place a bead in front of a slipped stitch. This makes the bead lie horizontally across the stitch on the right side of the work.

It is important to choose beads that are the appropriate size for the weight of yarn being used. Small delicate beads will look inadequate if used on a chunky yarn, just as large, heavy beads will look clumsy on a fine 4-ply yarn.

It is good fun to experiment with different-coloured yarns and beads to see what effects can be achieved. Black beads on black yarn can look very sophisticated, whereas red beads on a bright turquoise yarn can look quite dazzling. You can try threading two or three different-coloured beads onto a yarn in a particular order to create multi-coloured patterns. Once you start experimenting you will see that the possibilities are almost endless.

Small silver beads on a soft pastel yarn give this knitted fabric a special appeal that is both elegant and desirable.

Sequins

These can either be sewn onto knitting or knitted into a fabric. Knit in sequins using the slip stitch method in exactly the same way as for beads (see also above). The holes in sequins tend to be quite small, so this might limit you as to what weight of yarn you can use for your project.

As the sequins are knitted in they should be carefully stroked down so that they all lie flat and in one direction against the fabric. It is also worth noting that sequins will overlap each other if knitted in on every other stitch on every other row. And, depending on their size, each sequin might cover up to three stitches across the work.

This close placing of sequins on your knitting will create a wonderful shimmering fabric that looks very glamorous. Alternatively, sequins can look effective if used for motifs or horizontal stripes.

Buttons

These can be sewn onto your knitting after it is completed to add extra texture and colour to your design. Buttons come in a variety of shapes, colours and sizes and you can choose from many different types: plastic, wood, metal, pearl and shell are just a few examples.

The type of button that you choose for your project is important because it can completely change the whole mood of your design. For example, plastic buttons in solid, bright colours will give your project a contemporary feel, whereas pearl or shell buttons will add a touch of elegance and a more natural look. Think about what style you want to create before choosing your buttons.

It is interesting to experiment with mixing different types of buttons in one project. You could choose several different-coloured or different-sized buttons to give your knitting a really unique look.

Remember that buttons don't always have to be used as a fastening. They look great as decoration too. Where you place the buttons is totally up to you and, because they are sewn on rather than knitted in, you don't have to make this decision until you have finished knitting. You might want to sew them on in a regular all-over pattern, or maybe use them as an edging around the top of a bag or the hem of a garment.

Swiss darning

This technique uses a needle and separate length of yarn to simulate a knitted stitch on top of your knitted fabric. It is an easy way to add small amounts of colour to your work and it is also useful for getting around potentially tricky bits of a design, such as outlines around shapes or motifs. You can use your odds and ends of leftover yarn for this.

The yarn is taken through and around a knit stitch in such a way that it follows its shape perfectly and completely covers the stitch. Because Swiss darning is added to knitting after it has been completed, it can also be used to spice up a design if it needs an extra spot or two of colour to make it more appealing.

Combining techniques

With all of these different stitches and embellishments to choose from there are infinite possibilities at your fingertips. When several of these techniques are combined, knitting gets really exciting. All sorts of effects can be achieved through mixing colour with texture and embellishment.

Try knitting moss/seed stitch in multi-coloured stripes and you will see how the colours blend gently together to create a soft, muted effect. Or, if you work a single row of garter stitch on a wrong-side row of stocking/stockinette stitch at the same time as changing colour, a regular dotted line, like a line of stitching, will be created on the right side of the work.

Multi-colour intarsia and Fair Isle patterns can be given extra interest by introducing beads and textured stitches. Cables can be knitted in stripes of different colours or they can be beaded or embellished with embroidery, buttons or sequins to create spectacular-looking fabrics. These are just a few of the many possibilities you may want to try.

Remember that there are no rights or wrongs when you design a knitted fabric, so you can experiment as much as you like until you create something that you are really happy with. Always bear in mind your starting point – your original inspiration and the sketches that you made from it – because what you are creating in your knitting should be relating back to the ideas that first motivated you to design the project.

The detail of a heart motif is Swiss-darned onto a piece of knitting, which is sometimes a quicker and easier alternative to knitting it in.

Write it down

When you are experimenting keep a detailed written record of exactly how you create different stitches and patterns. There is nothing worse than developing a wonderful fabric that you can't re-knit because you don't remember how you created it.

What yarn to use

There is a wide range of yarns to choose from for your project, so you should take time to decide what yarn is going to be most suitable for your design.

Fibre types

Over the years knitters have become more experimental with materials and all sorts of things, from cut-up plastic bags to fuse wire, have been used to knit with. However, the most popular and more conventional types of knitting yarn can be split down into three main categories: animal, vegetable and synthetic.

Wool

This is very versatile, widely available and is the most popular fibre used in hand-knitting. Wool has a lot of elasticity and that makes it a great choice of yarn for textured stitch patterns such as cables and bobbles. It is also possible to felt knitted wool fabrics because the fibres are covered in tiny scales that matt together when they are agitated in warm, soapy water. Felted knitting can be cut into shapes and pieced together without fear of fraying.

Alpaca

Alpaca fleece is softer and lighter than wool, creating a very silky, fine-quality yarn. It is regarded as a luxury yarn and is usually more expensive than wool because the fleece takes much longer to grow than that of a sheep. Because of its high price tag it is usually spun to nothing heavier than a double knitting-weight (see page 29). When knitted up alpaca creates a soft, lightweight fabric that is slightly hairy, giving a soft, subtle look to both multi-coloured patterns (see pages 21–23) and textured stitches (see pages 16–20).

Mohair

This is quite a soft yarn, but it can sometimes be irritating to the skin because it is hairy. Therefore, it is often combined with other fibres, such as wool, to make it more comfortable to wear. Some mohair yarns are spun with a nylon binder to strengthen them because on its own pure mohair can be quite delicate. Mohair is durable, warm and lightweight and it creates a rather fuzzy and blurred-looking fabric that has little, if any, stitch definition. This means that it is not a great yarn to choose for textured stitches, but the surface of the knitting can be brushed to create beautiful blended colour effects.

Angora

This yarn is made from the hair of Angora rabbits and is incredibly soft and luxurious. The fibres are very short and slippery so they are usually mixed with other fibres to make the yarn stronger. It is also very expensive so it is used more for trims and edgings than for whole garments. Angora yarns have a wonderful silky-soft feel to them and a slightly blurred appearance when knitted. Therefore, delicate stitches and crisp lines of colour will look a bit fuzzy and have subtle stitch definition.

pure organic cotton

wool/cotton mix

pure wool

pure merino wool

mohair/silk mix

pure alpaca

alpaca/wool mix

pure merino wool

tweed wool

nylon/acrylic/wool/alpaca mix

cashmere/wool mix

loosely spun virgin wool

Soft, pure merino wool has a lot of elasticity and is a popular choice for hand-knitting because of its versatility.

Cashmere

Probably the most luxurious and expensive yarn you can buy. Cashmere fabrics are very soft and beautiful to touch, and they are lightweight and warm to wear. The yarns are usually spun to either a 4-ply-weight or a double knitting-weight, resulting in fine, elegant fabrics that look stunning worked in delicate-textured cable or lace patterns. Sparkling beads, sequins (see pages 24–25) or embroidery can be added to cashmere fabrics to enhance their glamorous appeal.

Silk

Silk is an expensive fibre because the production process is a difficult one and the cocoons are fragile. But it does produce a very desirable yarn that is light in weight, strong and durable. Silk fibres, like cashmere, are usually spun only to finer weights and are sometimes mixed with other fibres to make the yarns less expensive or to give them extra texture. Silk yarns are ideal for delicate stitch work and they look really special when they are embellished (see pages 24–25).

Cotton

This is made in many different weights and textures. It is very strong and absorbs moisture well, making it perfect for summer knits. Cotton yarns create crisp-looking fabrics with excellent stitch definition, but because they have little elasticity, any irregularities in the knitting will show up. Care should be taken to make sure that the tension/gauge of the knitted fabric is kept consistent.

Linen

Linen has a high natural lustre and fabrics knitted in linen yarns have a beautiful drape and soft feel. Linen is also very absorbent, which, like cotton, makes it an excellent yarn to choose for a summer garment. Stitch definition is crisp and clean and its smooth, matt appearance lends itself well to colour work (see pages 21–23) and fancy stitches (see pages 16–20).

Bamboo

Bamboo yarn absorbs moisture well and create a knitted fabric that is cool and comfortable to wear. Bamboo fabrics have unique elasticity and drape beautifully, as well as being strong and durable. Sometimes the bamboo fibre is spun together with another cheaper fibre, such as cotton. This makes it not only more interesting to look at, but also helps to keep the price down, as pure bamboo yarns tend to be rather expensive.

Soybean

These yarns are very soft and smooth and have a natural lustre. Not only are soybean yarns comfortable against the skin, but they have good moisture absorption, great ventilation and are insulating, too. When knitted up their soft, slightly fuzzy appearance makes them an ideal yarn for subtle blended effects.

Synthetic

The production of these fibres for hand-knitting yarns has developed rapidly over recent years to create some of today's most sophisticated-looking yarns. Despite their strength, durability and hard-wearing qualities, synthetic yarns lack many of the properties of natural fibre yarns. Having said that, some of the fancy synthetic yarns can look very effective if used for trims and edgings.

A soft, fluffy mohair yarn contrasts beautifully against a smooth pure wool yarn, and would look and feel wonderful if combined together in one piece of knitting.

Mix it up

You could experiment with mixing different yarn fibres in your design to create more interesting fabrics. For example, a smooth cotton yarn used next to a fluffy mohair yarn will provide a great contrast in texture. And as long as the weight of the yarns you are using is approximately the same, you can combine whatever you like to create unique-looking fabrics

Yarn types

There is a huge range of smooth yarns to choose from but some spinners have developed fibres into textured, fancy yarns to create an even wider range of interesting and exciting yarns for hand-knitting. These fancy yarns can transform a plain stocking/stockinette stitch fabric into something that looks very complicated and special. Here are just a few examples.

Bouclé

These yarns have an uneven and bulky feel that is produced by twisting together two or three strands and feeding one of those strands into the machinery at a faster pace than the others so that it loops up and creates a curl. Often two or three different-coloured strands are mixed to produce multi-coloured yarns. Bouclé yarns look especially effective if they are knitted with smooth yarns because the loops and curls stand proud from the fabric, creating a difference in texture that can be very useful for some designs.

Slubbed

Such yarns vary in thickness along their length, resulting in knitted fabrics with an uneven surface. They can be combined with smooth yarns to create fabrics with subtle changes in texture.

Tweed

These yarns have coloured 'knops' added to the fibres as they are being spun to create multi-coloured yarns that are slightly textured. Some tweed yarns are very subtly coloured and can be used with other similar-coloured yarns to achieve gentle colour changes in knitting. Other tweeds are very brightly coloured and have several different-coloured knops added to them to create more vibrant, eye-catching effects.

Chenille

These yarns look and feel like a velvet fabric when they are knitted up. Short lengths of yarn or filament, called the 'pile', are trapped between two twisted threads to produce a softly furred yarn. With their unique look and feel, chenille yarns can be used to add a touch of luxury to knitted fabrics.

Ribbon

Ribbon yarns are not made from sewing ribbon, but are usually of a tubular construction. They come in various different widths and when they are knitted up they create a fabric with a slightly textured surface as they usually twist round on themselves when they are being knitted. Finer ribbon yarns are less likely to twist than wide ribbons and, if knitted carefully, they can create a flatter, smoother-looking fabric. Alternatively, ribbon yarn can be threaded through eyelets in a piece of knitting, resulting in a very feminine and pretty fabric.

Novelty

These yarns include fun fur and eyelash yarns and they come in all sorts of crazy colours and textures. Most of these yarns have poor stitch definition because they are usually very hairy or furry, so they look more effective if they are used in small amounts in a knitted fabric – maybe along edgings or for borders – rather than for intricate patterns.

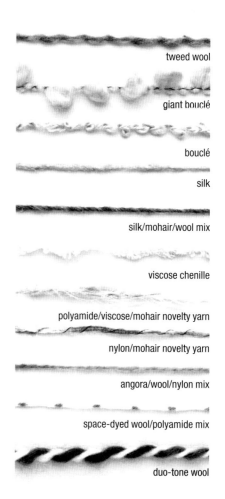

tweed wool

giant bouclé

bouclé

silk

silk/mohair/wool mix

viscose chenille

polyamide/viscose/mohair novelty yarn

nylon/mohair novelty yarn

angora/wool/nylon mix

space-dyed wool/polyamide mix

duo-tone wool

Yarn weights

Yarns are available in many different weights and these have been standardized so that they are universally understood. Finer-weight yarns create a more delicate and sophisticated look, whereas heavier-weight yarns tend to look more casual when knitted up.

Fabric quality

You need to think about how you want your knitted fabric to feel and behave (see page 57). Chunky yarns will create heavier, denser fabrics than finer yarns and so they work well when they are used for garments such as jackets and coats. Finer-weight yarns are more likely to drape well when they are knitted up and they are easier to shape, so these yarns are the best choice for garments such as skinny vest-tops or semi-fitted sweaters.

The amount of detail you can achieve in your knitted design is also influenced by the weight of yarn that you choose. This is because the heavier the yarn is, the less stitches and rows you will have to play with (see page 33). An intricate pattern with lots of detail will work best if it is knitted using a 4-ply yarn rather than a super chunky yarn.

Multi-coloured yarns

Some yarns are variegated in colour to offer an even wider range of options to the knitter. Random dyeing, also known as space-dyeing, creates a subtle blend of colours by partly immersing a hank of yarn in a series of dyes so that the colour varies throughout. Hand-painted yarns have dye applied directly to them, resulting in multi-coloured yarns that are usually rich in colour. Print-dyed yarns have colour applied to them by a mechanical process and consequently they have less gradual colour changes. Perhaps one of the most amazing inventions in recent times is self-patterning yarn that is dyed in specific lengths of colour so that it automatically creates stripes or patterns when it is knitted.

Another way to create blended effects is to knit using several different-coloured ends of yarn held together. As well as experimenting with colour, you can also mix different fibres to create unusual and unique-looking fabrics. You just need to remember that the weight of all the yarns used in your design must be similar so that the tension/gauge of the fabric is consistent (see page 52).

Colour change

The longer a yarn is in a dye bath the more likely it is that the physical quality of the yarn will be changed, meaning that it might knit up to a slightly different tension/gauge to other colours in the same range. So do knit a swatch in each colour yarn you choose, even if they are the same brand and type.

Yarn tension/gauge

The chart below shows the standard tension/gauge for the most popular weights of yarn, with the information given in both UK and American English terms.

Weight of yarn UK	Weight of yarn USA across 2.5 cm (1 in)	Average stitch tension/gauge to knit stocking/stockinette stitch	Average needle size required
4-ply	Fingering	6.75 sts–8 sts	2.75 mm–3.25 mm / US 2–US 3
Lightweight DK	Sport-weight	5.75 sts–6.5 sts	3.25 mm–3.75 mm / US 3–US 5
DK	DK	5.25 sts–6 sts	3.75 mm–4.50 mm / US 5–US 7
Aran	Worsted	4 sts–5 sts	4.50 mm–5.50 mm / US 7–US 9
Chunky	Chunky	3 sts–3.75 sts	5.50 mm–8.00 mm / US 9–US 11
Super chunky	Bulky	1.5 sts–2.75 sts	8.00 mm–15.00 mm / US 11–US 19

STEP **2** IDEAS ONTO PAPER

Working with proportional graph paper

The next step in the design process is to transfer your sketches onto proportional graph paper so that you can then knit a swatch.

Stocking/stockinette stitch, in any weight of yarn, always has a greater row tension/gauge than stitch tension, in other words, a stitch is wider than it is tall. So for knitting patterns, proportional graph paper – which you will find at the back of this book – is preferable to squared paper because it has been specially designed to imitate the shape of a knitted stitch, which is rectangular rather than square.

When you look at a piece of proportional graph paper you should see it as a piece of knitting, with each rectangle representing a stitch and each row of rectangles representing a row of knitting. Take care to use the paper the correct way around, otherwise the design will be distorted when it is knitted up. The rectangles must run horizontally across the page rather than vertically up and down it.

The really helpful thing about using proportional graph paper for knitting patterns is that it accurately shows what your design will look like when it is knitted. For example, if you draw a perfect circle onto proportional graph paper and knit it, you will achieve a perfect knitted circle. But if a perfect circle is drawn onto squared graph paper and knitted it will be an oval.

Getting it right

You need to decide whether you are going to knit your project in the conventional way from the cast-on (bottom) edge to the cast-off (top) edge, or in the less conventional way from side-to-side (see page 72). It is important to make this decision before you start working on the proportional graph paper because it will determine how you read the stitches and rows. If you knit your garment from cast-on to cast-off, the stitches will dictate width and the rows will dictate length. But if you work from side-to-side, the stitches will dictate length and the rows will dictate width.

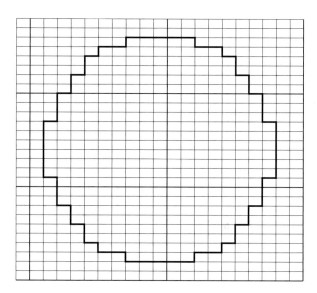

A circle drawn on proportional graph paper.

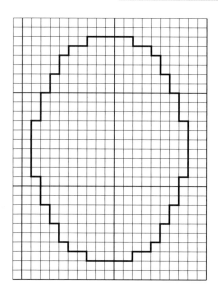

A circle drawn on normal graph paper.

Estimating tension/gauge

As you have not yet knitted a swatch (see page 50), it is most probable that when you are planning out your design on proportional graph paper you will not know the precise tension of your knitting. So you need to know how to work out the size of your design without a swatch.

The answer is to use an estimated tension that will enable you to make the necessary calculations. Information about tension is usually printed on the ball bands of knitting yarns and will be given over 10 cm (4 in) of stocking/stockinette stitch, unless otherwise stated.

If you don't have a ball band, another way to check the tension is to look at an existing knitting pattern that uses the same yarn as you have selected. However, you must check what stitch the tension is measured over because not all knitting patterns give the tension over stocking/stockinette stitch.

You can only use the tension given on a ball band or knitting pattern if your own design is knitted in the same stitch. This is because different stitch patterns and textures will knit up to a different number of stitches and rows to stocking/stockinette stitch (see pages 16–20).

It's a plan

If you use an estimated tension to plan out your design it may differ from your actual tension. So after you have tested your own tension (see page 52), you might need to make slight alterations to either the number of stitches and rows or to the patterns and motifs in your design to keep the finished measurements of your knitting correct.

Warm (40°C) Wool Cycle, minimum machine action	10 cm
Warm iron 160°C	10 cm / 36 rows
Do not bleach	28 sts
Dry cleanable in all solvents	10 UK
Do not tumble dry Dry flat out of direct sunlight	3¼ mm
	3 US
50 g Approx Length 183 m (200 yds)	100% Merino Wool 4PLY

These symbols are typical of what information can be found on the ball band of a knitting yarn.

Understanding scale

An important factor to consider when you are transferring your design onto proportional graph paper is scale – in other words, what the actual size of your design will be when it is knitted.

Scale depends on the weight of yarn that you are using for your project and the tension/gauge that it achieves. You need to think about this before you finalize your design ideas, otherwise you might find that your pattern or motif does not fit into your proposed design area (see page 45).

So, while you are working on your design it is important to be aware of how big the pattern or logo that you are drawing onto your chart will be when it is knitted so that you don't waste time working on something that you can't use because it is actually far too big or far too small. Therefore, it is a good idea to have a calculator beside you so that you can work out the actual measurements of your design as you are working on it. You could even plan out your design area first, so that you know exactly how many stitches and rows you have to play with. As long as you have an estimated tension/gauge to work with and you know the approximate finished size of your knitted panels, you can do this quite easily.

Working out the size of a square

Let's look at scale in a very simple way to understand how it works. If you draw a perfect square onto proportional graph paper it will not knit up to the same size as your drawing, unless the rectangles on the proportional graph paper are exactly the same size as your knitted stitches.

So how do you work out how big the square will be when it is knitted? A simple calculation based on tension/gauge will help you to determine this.

Calculating size

Width/horizontal measurement Divide the number of stitches in the design by the estimated stitch tension/gauge, then multiply this figure by 10 cm (4 in).
Length/vertical measurement Divide the number of rows in the design by the estimated row tension/gauge of your swatch, then multiply this figure by 10 cm (4 in). (If you are working from an actual tension/gauge rather than an estimated tension/gauge, then divide the number of stitches by this tension/gauge and multiply the figure by the measurement in cm (in) that you took across the swatch.)

Worked example: the sizes of two squares

To help you put this formula into practice, study this example.

A square 8 stitches wide and 12 rows deep is drawn onto proportional graph paper. (Although the numbers of stitches and rows are different, this shape will be a square when knitted up because the stitches are rectangular.)

A super chunky yarn is used to knit up the design. The tension/gauge of this yarn is 8 stitches and 12 rows to 10 cm (4 in).

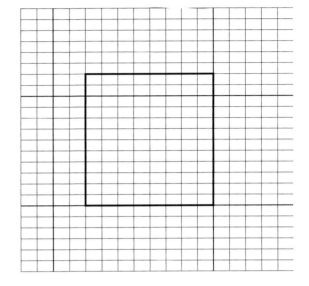

Width   8 stitches divided by 8 stitches = 1.
1 multiplied by 10 cm (4 in) = 10 cm (4 in).

Length   12 rows divided by 12 rows = 1.
1 multiplied by 10 cm (4 in) = 10 cm (4 in).

The square when knitted will measure
10 x 10 cm (4 x 4 in).

A smaller square 4 stitches wide and 6 rows deep is drawn onto proportional graph paper. (This is half the number of stitches and rows of the first square.) The same super chunky yarn and tension/gauge is used to knit up the design.

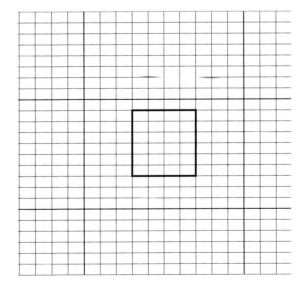

Width   4 stitches divided by 8 stitches = 0.5.
0.5 multiplied by 10 cm (4 in) = 5 cm (2 in).

Length   6 rows divided by 12 rows = 0.5.
0.5 multiplied by 10 cm (4 in) = 5 cm (2 in).

The square when knitted will measure
5 x 5 cm (2 x 2 in).

Simplifying your design

Some of the most successful designs turn out to be the simplest ones, so if your design is quite busy you may need to simplify it.

It may only become obvious that your design is too complex when you start knitting your swatch (see page 50). If this is the case you will need to go back to your graph, make some alterations and then knit another swatch. So it is good practice to take a break from your designing at frequent intervals to assess how it is looking and, if necessary, make some changes to your graph.

Drawing a curve on proportional graph paper

The exercise of simplifying shapes and motifs by re-drawing them onto proportional graph paper is common practice in knitwear design and you will have to do this if any of the original sketched lines cut across the rectangles on the proportional graph paper. This is because you are restricted to the shape of a knitted stitch, which we have already established is rectangular.

For example, if your sketch includes a smooth curve, this will have to be interpreted on the proportional graph paper as a jagged line that follows the edges of the rectangular stitch boxes. When this is knitted up it will look slightly irregular and so a little different from the original smooth curve.

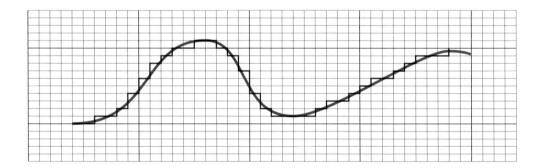

Squaring off a curve on proportional graph paper.

Making a design work in knitting

Unless your inspiration was originally completely geometric, you will almost always have to compromise a little bit on your design to make the sketched shapes and motifs work in knitting. But this is all part of the challenge of designing your own knitting patterns and shouldn't be considered a negative aspect.

The degree of compromise will also depend on the weight of yarn that you have chosen, because this is what dictates the size of the stitches and rows and consequently the number of stitches and rows in your design area.

If you are using a fine-weight yarn such as 4-ply you will be able to achieve a higher level of detail than if you use a chunky yarn, because you will have more stitches and rows to work with. So if your design is very intricate you are better off choosing a fine weight of yarn rather than a heavy one. This will allow you to include more detail in your knitting and curved lines will look a little bit smoother.

A chunky yarn has been used to knit up this multi-coloured scarf design, which results in large shapes and motifs with very little fine detail.

These cars have been knitted in a double-knitting weight yarn which has made it easier to include details such as the wheels, the windows and the smooth curve of the bonnet.

Pattern repeats

A pattern repeat can be coloured or it may be a textural pattern. Either way, your design will look more visually pleasing if each row begins and ends with a full repeat.

The number of stitches and rows in a panel may have to be altered to accommodate a specific pattern. Draw out one pattern repeat on proportional graph paper to see how many stitches and rows it involves. This will give you a multiple of stitches and rows for each pattern repeat that you can use in calculating the size of each knitted panel. The following suggestions for pattern repeats are for fabrics knitted on straight needles. If you are knitting your project in the round on circular or double-pointed needles you will not need to leave a stitch at each side edge for seam allowances. The pattern will simply continue around the panels as you work each round.

This Fair Isle pattern repeat will continue perfectly around your garment if the two selvedge edges are seamed together because it starts and finishes with a half pattern repeat.

Welts

A welt is a term used to describe a band or border on an edge of a knitted fabric. A welt is often ribbed, though it can be another firm stitch, such as moss or garter stitch.

Most welts, whether they are ribbed, cabled, beaded or multi-coloured, rely on a pattern repeat, and this will influence the number of stitches that you cast on and the number of rows that you knit. Remember that a stitch at each side edge of your knitting will be taken into a seam, unless it is a finished edge, as on a scarf. Therefore the first and last stitches of each row should not be included in the pattern repeat.

Pattern plan

When planning out pattern repeats on a project that has two panels with shaped sides (see page 98) it is important to think how the design will look when the panels are joined. It is most likely that the pattern repeat will not meet up correctly on the side seams and with some projects this can look disastrous. If this is the case, it might be a good idea to re-consider the shape of the panels and make the sides of the knitting straight instead of shaped.

Single (1 x 1) rib welt

To make the pattern repeat work on panels that are going to be seamed together, cast on an even number of stitches. Begin all rows with K1 and end with P1. Do the same on both panels and when they are seamed together the K1, P1 rib pattern will continue perfectly across the seam.

To make the pattern repeat work on a panel that is not going to be seamed, an odd number of stitches should be cast on. Begin and end all right-side rows with K1 and begin and end all wrong-side rows with P1 (see also page 18).

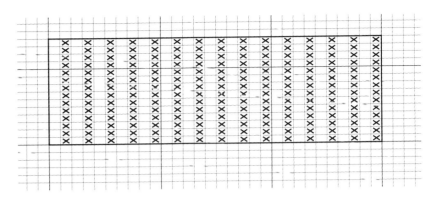

Single (1 x 1) rib pattern repeat drawn onto proportional graph paper for panels that are going to be seamed together.

Double (2 x 2) rib welt

To make the pattern repeat work on panels that are going to be seamed together, begin all right-side and wrong-side rows with K3 and end with P3. When the two panels are seamed together the extra knit stitch and purl stitch at either end of the knitting will be taken into the seam, and the K2, P2 rib pattern will continue perfectly across the seam.

To make the pattern repeat work on a panel that is not going to be seamed, begin and end all right-side rows with K2, and begin and end all wrong-side rows with P2.

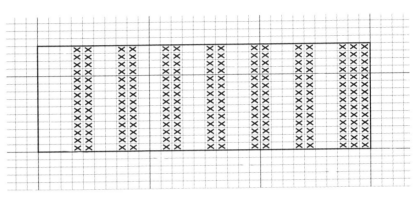

Double (2 x 2) pattern repeat drawn onto proportional graph paper for panels that are going to be seamed together.

Moss/seed stitch welt

To make the pattern repeat work on panels that are going to be seamed together, cast on an even number of stitches. Begin all right-side rows with K1 and end with P1, and begin all wrong-side rows with P1 and end with K1. When the two panels are seamed together the moss/seed stitch pattern will continue perfectly across the seam.

To make the pattern repeat work on a panel that is not going to be seamed, cast on an odd number of stitches and begin and end all right-side and wrong-side rows with K1 (see also page 17).

Garter stitch welt

Any number of stitches can be cast on and the pattern will work across both seamed and single panels (see also page 16).

Textured patterns

A variety of stitches may be used for the main body of the knitting, including knit and purl patterns, basketweave, slip stitch patterns and bobbles (see pages 16–20). The number of stitches and rows in a textured pattern repeat will vary from one design to another, so the best way to see how to make the repeat work is to plan it out on proportional graph paper. Once you have established how many stitches and rows are in one repeat, you can divide them into the total number of stitches and rows in your design area (see page 45).

However, it is quite probable that the pattern repeat will not fit perfectly into your design area and, if this is the case, a compromise will have to be made. You will have to either increase or decrease the number of stitches and rows in your design area, or you will have to alter the number of stitches and rows in the pattern repeat itself. In most cases it is probably easier to compromise on the design area and make it slightly longer, shorter, narrower or wider.

Another solution is to begin and end a pattern repeat on a half repeat rather than a full one (see page 38). Then, if two panels are going to be seamed together, the two half-repeats will meet on the side seams and create one full repeat. A half-pattern repeat can also look pleasing on the edges of a single panel with no seams.

Cable patterns

Cabled fabrics are always narrower in width than stocking/stockinette stitch fabrics because a cable pattern pulls in the stitches when they are crossed over each other. Therefore, extra stitches are usually added at the beginning of a cable pattern to accommodate this decrease in width. This is the first thing that should be considered when you are planning out a cable design (see also page 19).

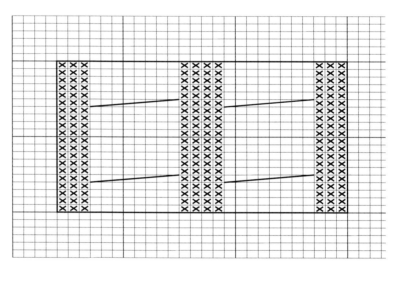

Cable pattern repeat drawn onto proportional graph paper for panels that are going to be seamed together.

Take an example of a pattern repeat of C8B (cable eight stitches back), with four stitches knitted in reverse stocking/stockinette stitch between each cable. The cable pattern starts after a section of stocking/stockinette stitch has been knitted.

The increases are made into the stitches that cross over each other to make the cable twists, not into the stitches between cables. The total number of stitches needed for each cable is increased from half that number in the stocking/stockinette stitch.

So, in this example of C8B, the eight stitches in the cable should start from four stocking/stockinette stitches and an increase should be made into each of them bringing the number of stitches up to the eight needed for the cable.

The easiest way to work out a cable pattern repeat is to plan it on proportional graph paper. Pencil in the stitches where the cable is to be knitted and the stitches between the cable. Make a note of how many stitches each cable needs and how many these will be increased from and then you can work out the total number of stitches for one pattern repeat.

Cables from a cast-on edge The same principle applies for cables that come directly from a cast-on edge. Cast on the required number of stitches for the width of the panel. In the first row of knitting, increase into the stitches as required to create the extra stitches needed for each cable.

If the cables continue right up to the cast-off, then in the last row of knitting, decrease the stitches forming each cable to half their number. Then cast/bind off all the stitches across the panel. These techniques prevent the cast-on and cast/bind-off edges from ruffling where the cables begin and end.

Cables across a seam Cables look really professional when they form a continuous pattern across a seam joining two panels. But to achieve this, careful planning of how to begin and end each row is required. Using the same example of C8B as before, the stitches could be set as follows.

Begin all right-side rows with P3, followed by a pattern repeat of K8 for each cable and P4 for the stitches in between. End each right-side row with P3. Begin all wrong-side rows with K3, followed by a pattern repeat of P8 for each cable and K4 for the stitches in between. End each wrong-side row with K3. When the two panels are seamed together one stitch at each side will be taken into the seam and the reverse stocking/stockinette stitch between the cables will continue perfectly across the seam (see illustration, left).

Lace patterns

These patterns are created by increasing and decreasing stitches within a repeat, so it is important to make sure that each row begins and ends with a full pattern repeat (see also page 20). When each row has been completed there must be the correct number of stitches on the needle. This applies to both single panels of knitting and panels that are going to be joined.

It is quite easy to plan out a lace repeat on a project that doesn't have any shaping at the edges, and drawing the pattern repeats onto proportional graph paper will help you to fit them into the design area.

Lace pattern repeat drawn onto proportional graph paper for panels that are going to be seamed together.

Shaping lace When the edges of a project are shaped, planning the pattern repeats becomes more complicated. The easiest method is to work increased stitches at the edges using stocking/stockinette stitch or reverse stocking/stockinette stitch. When enough have been increased, work a full pattern repeat across them on subsequent rows. The same principle applies to decreases: as stitches are decreased at an edge, work the reminder of the repeat that has been decreased into in stocking/stockinette stitch or reverse stocking/stockinette stitch. This might make the side edges of the knitting look a little dense, but there really isn't any other way around it. The number of increases in a pattern repeat must be balanced by the number of decreases to keep the number of stitches correct, so you cannot work only part of a repeat because the number of stitches will be incorrect.

Also consider the number of rows in a lace pattern repeat. It may be more pleasing if the knitting ends after a full pattern repeat has been completed.

Coloured patterns

From simple horizontal stripes to detailed Fair Isle patterns, colour work can be a really effective tool in knitting design.

Fair Isle and intarsia patterns

The pattern repeats for both these types of colour knitting can also be effectively planned out on proportional graph paper (see also page 32). Make the repeats fit into the design area using the same principles as for textured patterns (see page 40). Remember to add an extra stitch to each side for the seam allowances if the panels are to be joined.

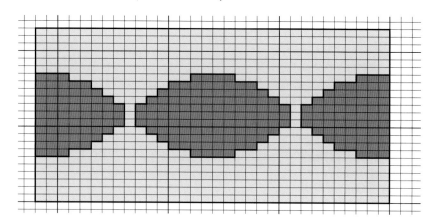

Intarsia pattern repeat drawn onto proportional graph paper for panels that are going to be seamed together.

Horizontal stripes

Horizontal stripe patterns don't usually have a pattern repeat across the knitting, unless they are textured. If this is the case, follow the suggestion for beginning and ending rows given for textured patterns (see page 40) so that the texture fits perfectly into the number of stitches.

Most horizontal stripe patterns have a vertical repeat instead. So the number of rows involved in each pattern repeat going up the knitting needs to be worked out so that the stripe pattern begins and finishes exactly as you want it to.

Vertical stripes

Most vertical stripe patterns with the stripes knitted in intarsia across the work will have a repeat across the knitting, but probably not up the knitting. If two panels are going to be joined together it is important to consider how the stripe pattern will look where it meets on the side seams.

If both panels begin and end with the same colour stripe this will create a large block of one colour at the side edges, and this usually looks very displeasing. So to avoid this it is essential to plan out the stripe pattern so that

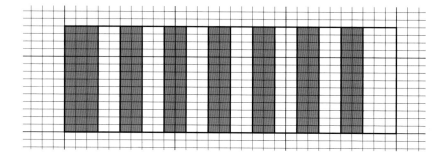

Vertical stripe pattern drawn onto proportional graph paper for panels that are going to be seamed together.

the panels begin and end with a different-colour stripe. For example, on a two-colour stripe pattern using red and white, both panels would have to begin with a red stripe and end with a white stripe. Then when the two panels are joined together the red-and-white stripes will continue perfectly across the seam.

On single panels of knitting that are not going to be seamed, a vertical stripe repeat usually looks better if it begins and ends with the same colour stripe. This might mean planning out a stripe pattern that works from the centre out towards each edge, rather than as a multiple across the fabric.

Centring a motif

If you need to place a motif in the centre of your knitting it is easiest to work this out on proportional graph paper (see page 32). First of all you need to consider how many stitches the motif will take up across the knitting, because this will influence how many stitches you will need to cast on for the whole panel.

If the motif is an odd number of stitches across, you will need to cast on an odd number of stitches to centre it. But if the motif is an even number of stitches across, you will need to cast on an even number of stitches to centre it.

You will also have to consider the number of rows in your design area and make sure that there is the same number of rows above the motif as there are below it.

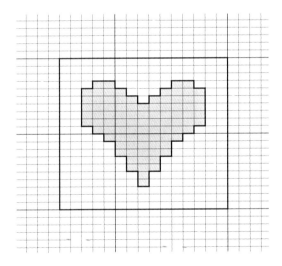

A motif centralized on proportional graph paper.

Embellished patterns

Embellishments can be sewn onto your knitting after it is finished, in which case, though some planning is needed, the final positioning can be worked out once the project is completed and sewn up. However, if you are knitting in embellishments, then all the planning needs to be done before you start work.

Bead and sequin patterns

These pattern repeats can be planned out onto proportional graph paper and the principles for making textured pattern repeats fit (see page 40) can be used equally well for bead and sequin patterns.

However, on panels that are going to be joined together, a bead or sequin must not be knitted in on either the first or last stitch of a row because it will get trapped in the seam. If the slip-stitch method of knitting in beads and sequins is used, it is actually technically impossible to do this anyway.

Converting measurements into stitches and rows

To transfer your drawings on proportional graph paper into a piece of knitting it is essential you understand how the number of stitches and rows are calculated.

Earlier on in this chapter you were shown how to calculate size (width and length) from stitch and row tensions/gauges (see page 33). Now you need the calculations for working out the number of stitches and rows required to create a specific measurement.

This formula for working out the number of stitches and rows needed is absolutely fundamental to your designing and will be used to calculate all of the measurements of your project.

Calculating stitches and rows

Width Divide the required width measurement by 10 cm (4 in), then multiply this figure by the estimated stitch tension/gauge.

Length Divide the required length measurement by 10 cm (4 in), then multiply this figure by the estimated row tension/gauge.

(If you are working from an actual tension/gauge rather than an estimated tension/gauge, then divide the number of stitches by this tension/gauge and multiply the figure by the measurement in cm (in) that you took across the swatch.)

Worked example: the size of a blanket

To help you put this formula into practice, study this example. You want to knit a baby blanket that will measure 50 x 50 cm (20 x 20 in). A double knitting-weight yarn will be used to knit the blanket. The tension/gauge of this yarn is 22 stitches and 30 rows to 10 cm (4 in).

Using the formula given above, the measurements of the blanket are calculated as follows:

Width   50 cm (20 in) divided by 10 cm (4 in) = 5. 5 multiplied by 22 (stitch tension/gauge) = 110 stitches.

Length   50 cm (20 in) divided by 10 cm (4 in) = 5. 5 multiplied by 30 (row tension/gauge) = 150 rows.

Therefore, you need to cast on 110 stitches and knit 150 rows to make a blanket that measures 50 x 50 cm (20 x 20 in).

Sketch of a knitted blanket measuring 50 x 50 cm (20 x 20 in)

Planning out a design area

The design area is the space (in stitches and rows) that you will draw out onto proportional graph paper and plan your design into. To calculate your design area you will need to know what size you want your knitted panel/s to be.

As you haven't knitted a swatch yet (see page 50), you will need to base the calculations for your design area on an estimated tension/gauge (see page 33) for the yarn you have chosen.

Decide approximately what size, in either centimetres or inches, you want your knitted panel/s to be and use the formula given for calculating stitches and rows (see page 44) and the estimated tension/gauge to work out the size of your design area. Map this out onto proportional graph paper, then draw in any details such as pattern repeats or motifs to check that they fit into the stitches and rows you have calculated.

Remember that it is not crucial at this point to have decided on the exact measurements of your knitted panels because this will be finalized and probably re-calculated when you knit a swatch and make a spec drawing (see page 60) of your design later on. But this exercise will give you a good idea of what your design will look like and how many stitches and rows you will need.

Worked example: fitting a repeat pattern across the width of a sweater panel

This example will help you understand how you fit a horizontal repeat pattern into a designated design area. The width of the sweater front measures 50 cm (20 in). An Aran weight yarn will be used to knit up the sweater. The tension/gauge of this yarn is 18 sts and 24 rows to 10 cm (4 in). The repeat pattern is 15 sts across.

Width of the sweater   50 cm (20 in) multiplied by 18 (stitch tension/gauge)

= 900 (360) divided by 10 cm (4 in) = 90 sts

90 sts divided by 15 (sts in the pattern repeat)

= 6

Therefore, you can fit 6 repeats of the pattern across the width of the sweater.

STEP 3 KNITTING A SWATCH

Why knit a swatch?

Knitting a swatch is a crucial part of the design process. There are four important reasons for knitting one and they are explained here.

To check tension/gauge

Tension/gauge is the stitch size you create when you knit. We all hold yarn and needles in a different way and this creates variations in tension/gauge between knitters. Also, it is a good idea to knit your swatch when you are in a relaxed mood. A stressed knitter may be knitting considerably more tightly than usual and so their true tension/gauge will not be recorded. However, the main influence on your tension/gauge is the size of needles you use.

The stitch and row tensions/gauges of your swatch are the basis for the mathematical calculations that you need to do to plan out your design. You cannot move on in the design process without measuring your tension/gauge.

It is risky just to use the average tension/gauge given on the ball-band of your yarn, because your own tension/gauge may differ from it, especially if your design is in a textured stitch, embellished or multi-coloured.

A knitted swatch is an essential part of the design process and is crucial to calculating the number of stitches and rows you need in your design.

To test your design

On paper your design might look amazing, but what will it look like when it is knitted? By knitting a swatch you can test out every aspect of your design and check that your ideas are translating into knitting in the way that you want them to. Any textured stitches, colour combinations or patterns and motifs should be swatched so that you can evaluate your ideas and decide whether or not the design is working.

To test fabric quality

The size of needles that you knit your swatch with will influence the quality of the fabric. So you need to decide how you want the fabric to feel and behave and then you need to choose the correct needle size to achieve the quality you want (see page 57). Do you want the fabric to be quite open and loose, or do you want it be more stable? Does the fabric need to drape and flow, or does it need to be firm?

To calculate yarn quantity

You will need to know how much yarn to buy to knit your project and your swatch will help you to calculate this. If your design is multi-coloured, weigh all the balls of yarn that you use for your swatch before you start and when you have completed your swatch. Write down the difference in weight for each colour. For a one-colour design you simply need to weigh the swatch itself. How to calculate the amount of yarn for your project using these recorded weights is explained in Step 5 (see pages 78–80).

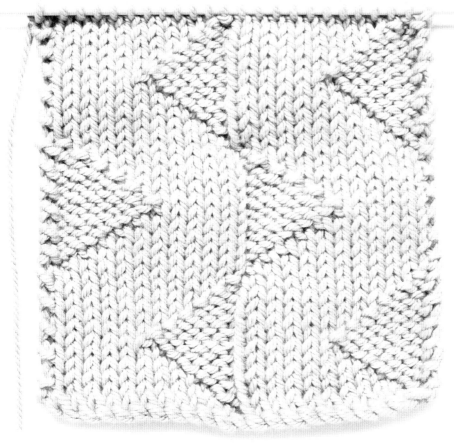

Your swatch is a realization of your design and will show you whether or not your ideas are working.

Knitting a swatch correctly

It is really important that your swatch is knitted correctly so that you can measure the tension/gauge easily and record it accurately.

Not every knitting pattern gives clear instructions on how to knit a proper swatch, so many knitters do not knit one in the right way and this can have disastrous consequences. An inaccurate tension/gauge reading can result in your project knitting up too big or too small, or too long or too short (see pages 54–55). So the first tip for knitting a swatch is to make sure that you cast on a sufficient number of stitches and work enough rows.

Calculating the number of stitches and rows for a swatch

At this stage you do not know what your stitch or row tension/gauge is, so as a starting point you need to base it on an estimate (see also page 33). Look at the ball band of the yarn you are using, or at a pattern that uses the same yarn, and it will tell you the number and stitches and rows to 10 cm (4 in). Add at least half the number of stitches and half the number of rows to the given quantities so that your swatch will measure approximately 15 x 15 cm (6 x 6 in) when finished.

Worked example: stitches and rows for a swatch

Tension/gauge on yarn ball band is 22 stitches and 30 rows to 10 cm (4 in).

22 stitches divided by 2 = 11 stitches.

30 rows divided by 2 = 15 rows.

Add 11 to 22 and cast on 33 stitches.

Add 15 to 30 and work 45 rows.

Swatch size

The swatch needs to be larger than the measurement you are going to take from it because the edge stitches on both sides are tighter and sit closer together than the stitches in the middle of the knitting. The cast-on edge at the bottom will pull in gently and distort both the stitches and the rows. So, to get a precise tension/gauge, the stitches and rows must be measured within the swatch, not from edge to edge.

Swatch pattern

The other important point about knitting a swatch is that you must knit it in the stitch and pattern of your design. There is no point in knitting up a plain piece of stocking/stockinette stitch if your design is in a textured stitch because the tensions/gauges of the two fabrics may well be different. What you need to do is to take a small section from your design and knit it up as your swatch.

If your design has an all-over pattern repeat, then knit your whole swatch in this repeat design. If your design has placed motifs or patterns in it, you need to include pattern. And if your design has a mixture of different-textured stitches or patterns, then you will have to knit a cross-section that shows all of them.

With this type of design it might even be worth knitting up the different stitches and patterns in several separate swatches. You might find that the tension/gauge differs between them and consequently you might have to change your needle size for different parts of the design to maintain a consistent tension/gauge. This can be so with stitches such as moss/seed stitch or garter stitch (see pages 16–17), which condense the rows and spread out the stitches in comparison to stocking/stockinette stitch.

Casting off

When you have finished knitting, cast/bind off the stitches loosely to avoid them pulling in along the top edge and distorting the shape of the swatch. Alternatively, carefully slip the stitches off the knitting needle and leave them unfinished so that the knitting sits at its natural width.

Swatching welts

It is not always necessary to test the tension/gauge of a welt at the bottom edge of a garment, unless it is going to affect the rest of the stitches in the design. Instead, plan the depth of the welt in centimetres (inches) on your spec (see page 66), then work out the number of rows necessary to achieve it.

Your swatch must sample all of the stitch patterns and use the same knitting techniques that you plan to include in your final design.

Swatch techniques

As well as using the same stitches, use the same techniques to knit your swatch as you will use to knit your actual project. For example, if your design is a Fair Isle pattern, make a note of whether you stranded yarns across the back of the work or whether you wove them in every other stitch. Different techniques can create variations in tension/gauge and can upset the final calculations for your knitted panels.

Measuring tension/gauge

Decide whether you are going to work in centimetres or inches and stick to whatever you choose for all the measurements and calculations that you do for your design. Mixing the two types of measurement only leads to confusion and inevitably mistakes will be made.

To take an accurate measurement it is best to measure the stitches and rows across 10 cm (4 in), a measurement that will fit comfortably within your swatch without touching the edges. If you have knitted your swatch in a fluffy or an uneven, textured yarn it is a good idea to measure the tension/gauge at several different points across the knitting and then record the average.

Tension/gauge should be measured across a swatch that is in its finished state, so if it has been knitted in a yarn that needs pressing, press the swatch following the guidelines on the ball band. After pressing, the edges should be fairly flat and easy to see, which means that you shouldn't have to pin out the swatch to measure it.

Lay the swatch on a hard, flat surface, such as a table or worktop. This should ensure that the knitting is at its natural width and is not distorted by what is underneath it. Make sure that the right side of the knitting is face-up.

Pinning out a swatch

If you have used a yarn that must not be pressed, you may have to pin the swatch out before measuring it to keep it flat and even. To do this, lay the swatch right-side up on an ironing board. Ease it into shape, being very careful not to stretch it in any direction and so distort the stitches and rows. Push pins through the edge stitches and through the cast-on and cast/bind-off rows to pin the swatch to the ironing board.

The right equipment

If you have a lamp or a spotlight, it is a good idea to position this near you so that you can see the individual stitches and rows clearly without straining your eyes. Alternatively, try to work close to a window so that natural daylight helps your vision.

The best tool to use to measure tension/gauge is a clear plastic ruler. A tape measure is flexible and doesn't lie flat as easily as a hard ruler does.

Recognizing stitches

Before you measure your tension/gauge you must understand what both a knit and a purl stitch look like. Look closely at your knitting and familiarize yourself with the stitches, because to count them accurately you need to recognize their shape.

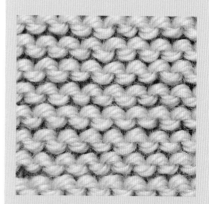

A purl stitch is curved, like a wave.

A knit stitch is a V-shape.

Counting stitches

Lay the ruler across the stitches in the swatch so that 10 cm (4 in) sits comfortably within the edges. Mark out 10 cm (4 in) with a pin at each end of the measurement and then remove the ruler and count the number of stitches between the pins.

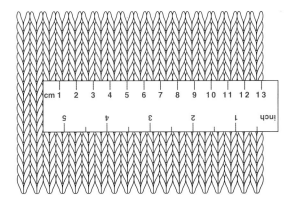

Using a ruler to measure stitch tension/gauge across a swatch.

Counting rows

Now count the number of rows by repeating this process, but lay the ruler down the middle of the knitting instead, making sure that 10 cm (4 in) fits easily between the cast-on and cast/bind-off edges of the swatch.

On the wrong side of stocking/stockinette stitch each row looks like a continuous wave. If you think that the rows will be easier to count on this side, lay the swatch with the wrong side face up and measure the tension/gauge as before.

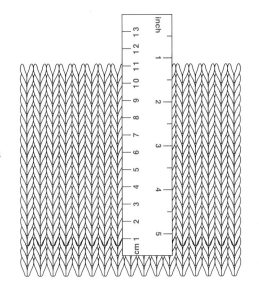

Using a ruler to measure row tension/gauge down a swatch.

Using stitch markers

If your swatch is knitted in a yarn that has very poor stitch definition, or in a fancy stitch such as cable or lace where the individual stitches and rows are difficult to see, you may need to use stitch markers to measure out the stitches and rows.

Work about 2.5 cm (1 in) of the knitted pattern, then place a stitch marker in the middle of the row you are knitting. Count each row worked after this marker. When you have worked about another 5 cm (2 in), place a second marker a few stitches in from the edge of the knitting. Work across the row, counting the stitches as you go.

When you have worked 10 cm (4 in) across the row (keep checking the measurement with the ruler until it is correct), place a third marker, then complete the row. Continue to work the swatch, counting the rows, until you have worked 10 cm (4 in) in length. Place a fourth and final marker.

The number of stitches between the vertical markers is your stitch tension/gauge, and the number of rows between the horizontal markers is your row tension/gauge.

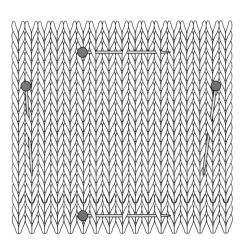

Using markers to measure tension/gauge.

Recording tension/gauge

Having taken the time to knit and measure your swatch properly, it's important to record the results accurately or the whole exercise will be in vain.

When you are counting the stitches and rows in your swatch it is essential that you record the exact number, even if it is a half stitch or row. This is because when the tensions/gauges are multiplied up to calculate the stitches and rows needed for your knitted panels, any discrepancies will be exaggerated. The following examples show how an inaccurate tension/gauge reading can affect the final measurements of panels.

Worked example: multiplying tensions/gauges correctly
The actual tension/gauge of the swatch is 17.5 stitches and 23.5 rows to 10 cm (4 in).
The desired size of the knitted panel is 50 x 50 cm (20 x 20 in).

Stitch tension/gauge (width) 50 cm (20 in) (panel size) divided by 10 cm (4 in) (swatch size) = 5.
5 multiplied by 17.5 (stitch tension/gauge) = 87.5 stitches,
which has to be rounded to a whole number, so 88 stitches.

Row tension/gauge (length) 50 cm (20 in) (panel size) divided by 10 cm (4 in) (swatch size) = 5
5 multiplied by 23.5 (row tension/gauge) = 117.5 rows,
which has to be rounded to a whole number, so 118 rows.

Therefore, if 88 stitches are cast on and 118 rows are knitted, the panel will measure the required 50 x 50 cm (20 x 20 in).

Worked example: multiplying tensions/gauges incorrectly
If the swatch tension/gauge is rounded up to 18 stitches and 24 rows and the same calculation is made, 90 stitches will be cast on and 120 rows will be knitted. This may not sound much, just an extra two stitches and two rows, but this calculation shows how the finished measurements will vary.

Swatch stitch tension/gauge 17.5 stitches = 10 cm (4 in), so 1 stitch = 0.57 cm (0.23 in).
90 (stitches cast on) x 0.57 cm (0.23 in) = 51.3 cm (20.7 in).

Swatch row tension/gauge 23.5 rows = 10 cm (4 in), so 1 row = 0.43 cm (0.17 in).
120 (rows knitted) x 0.43 cm (0.17 in) = 51.6 cm (20.4 in).

Therefore the finished panel of 90 stitches by 120 rows will measure 51.3 cm (20.7 in) wide by 51.6 cm (20.4 in) long.

The difference in width measurement is 1.3 cm (0.5 or ½ in).
The difference in length measurement is 1.6 cm (0.7 or about ⅝ in).

Differences in measurements

Though the differences in measurement between the two examples are not large, remember that the difference in width will be doubled if a back and front panel are knitted and sewn together to make a garment. Here, the difference in width around the body will be plus 2.5 cm (1 in) in total.

On a loose-fitting garment this will probably be less of an issue, but on a fitted garment this difference in tension/gauge can mean that the garment will be too big and the whole project can be a disaster.

It is worth noting that this difference in measurement came from only a half stitch and half a row being rounded up. So if the tension/gauge is recorded more incorrectly than this, the difference in measurement will be greater and the results even more disappointing.

Noting results

When you have counted the number of stitches and rows to 10 cm (4 in), write down the figures in a notebook. Also make a note of the yarn that you used and the size of the knitting needles, so if you use the same yarn for another project you will already have both the tension/gauge and the needle size worked out.

Record the weight and size of the finished swatch in your notebook so that later on in the design process you can work out the amount of yarn you will need to knit your project (see pages 78–80).

It is important to maintain a regular tension/gauge if knitting in the round or on straight needles, otherwise the resulting fabric will look uneven and the project may not fit as well as you want it to.

Take note

Start a knitting journal so that you can record all of the projects you knit. Make notes of all the important points about your projects, such as type of yarn used, size of knitting needles, how many balls of yarn a project used and how long it took to knit. It is also a good idea to take a photograph of each completed project and keep them with the notes you have made, then you will have your very own historical reference of everything that you have knitted.

Is the design working?

When you are knitting your swatch it is important to stop at frequent intervals to evaluate your design. You need to be very honest with yourself at this stage and question whether what you are creating is what you want.

It is sometimes very difficult to be critical of your own work – especially when you have been focusing on it for a long time. So step away from your knitting for a short while, take a break and then look at it again later on with fresh eyes.

Asking questions

If you feel that your design is working well and you are happy with it, then this is good news because you can continue to knit your swatch and complete it. But if you are not pleased with your design, changes will have to be made. Ask yourself questions to help you decide what you need to change to improve it.

• Are the colours working together?
• Do you need to add extra colours to spice up the design?
• Does the pattern look balanced?
• Is it too complicated?
• Does the design need some added embellishment?

If asking these questions does not give you a solution to your design problem, the next step is to go back and look again at your original inspiration and the sketches you made from it. You may then decide to re-draw your ideas onto proportional graph paper (see page 32) and start another swatch.

    Re-knitting your swatch should not be seen a step backwards in the design process. In fact, it is common practice for most designers to knit several swatches before they are happy with the results. Each swatch that you knit should be kept as a record of the development of your design so that you can see the progress you have made.

There is no point in continuing with your swatch if you are not happy with how it is looking. So it is a good idea to evaluate your knitting at regular intervals.

Getting the right fabric quality

Fabric quality is controlled by the size of knitting needles you use, so you need to make sure that you have chosen the right size needles to knit your swatch.

As a basic guide, if you choose a needle that is smaller than the recommended size for the yarn that you are using, the yarn will knit up tighter and create a firmer fabric. Conversely, if you choose a needle that is larger than the recommended size, the yarn will knit up more openly and create a looser fabric.

So before knitting your swatch you need to decide what your project is going to be, because this will help you to determine how you want the fabric to feel and behave.

Garment fabrics

If you want to knit a garment then you will need to decide whether you want the fabric to drape and be fluid, or whether you want it to be more stable.

Loose-fitting sweaters, tunics and cardigans will fit comfortably around the body if they are knitted to an average tension/gauge, whereas a coat or jacket will benefit from being knitted more tightly. A tight tension/gauge will create a firmer fabric that is less likely to stretch or drop and this is especially important if you are knitting something heavy, such as a long coat.

Accessory fabrics

Items such as bags, blankets and cushions also work well if they are knitted to a tight tension/gauge. Accessories that are worn on the body, such as scarves and hats, need to have more stretch and can be knitted more loosely.

Try different needles

You might need to try out several different needle sizes before you decide on the best size for your project. If you already have a good idea of your own natural tension/gauge, making a needle selection is easier. Start by looking at the ball band of the yarn that you are using and see what needle size is recommended.

Finer yarns, such as 4-ply, will recommend a thinner needle, maybe 3 mm, and bulkier yarns will recommend a thicker needle, maybe 8 mm. Although most yarns fall into specific weight categories (see page 29), there are still variations in tension/gauge and appropriate needle size between yarns within a category, so make sure that you check the ball band information carefully.

If you want your swatch to knit up to an average tension/gauge, start off by using the needle size recommended on the ball band. If you know that you usually achieve a correct pattern tension/gauge, then you will probably not have to try out any other needle sizes.

If you do experiment with different needle sizes before you decide which you like best, keep all of your samples because these can be handy for other projects. Make sure that you label them so that you know what needle size you used for each project.

Knitting needles are made from all sorts of materials, such as nickel and bamboo. Choose to knit with the needles that you like the feel of best and result in the most pleasing tension/gauge.

STEP 4 MAPPING OUT THE DESIGN

The specification drawing

The starting point for working out the stitches and rows for any design is a specification drawing, also referred to as a 'spec drawing'. This is a basic diagram that shows the shape of each knitted panel.

What to include on your drawing

All of the measurements of the panels are written on the spec drawing. For a sweater design, the back, front and one sleeve will be illustrated. Only when all of the measurements have been decided can the stitches and rows for your design be calculated. Indicate on the spec drawing where any motifs, patterns or fancy stitches are going to be so that you can see how they look in relation to the whole design.

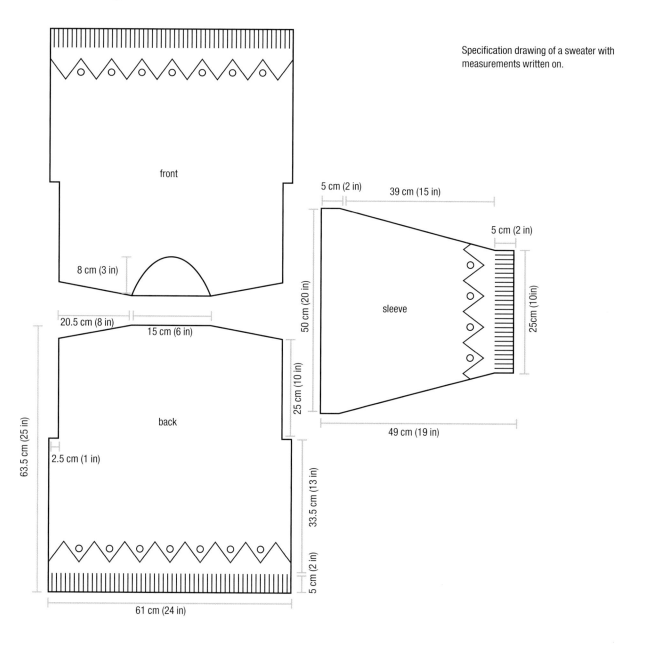

Specification drawing of a sweater with measurements written on.

front

5 cm (2 in)   39 cm (15 in)

5 cm (2 in)

8 cm (3 in)

50 cm (20 in)

sleeve

25cm (10in)

20.5 cm (8 in)

15 cm (6 in)

25 cm (10 in)

63.5 cm (25 in)

back

2.5 cm (1 in)

49 cm (19 in)

33.5 cm (13 in)

5 cm (2 in)

61 cm (24 in)

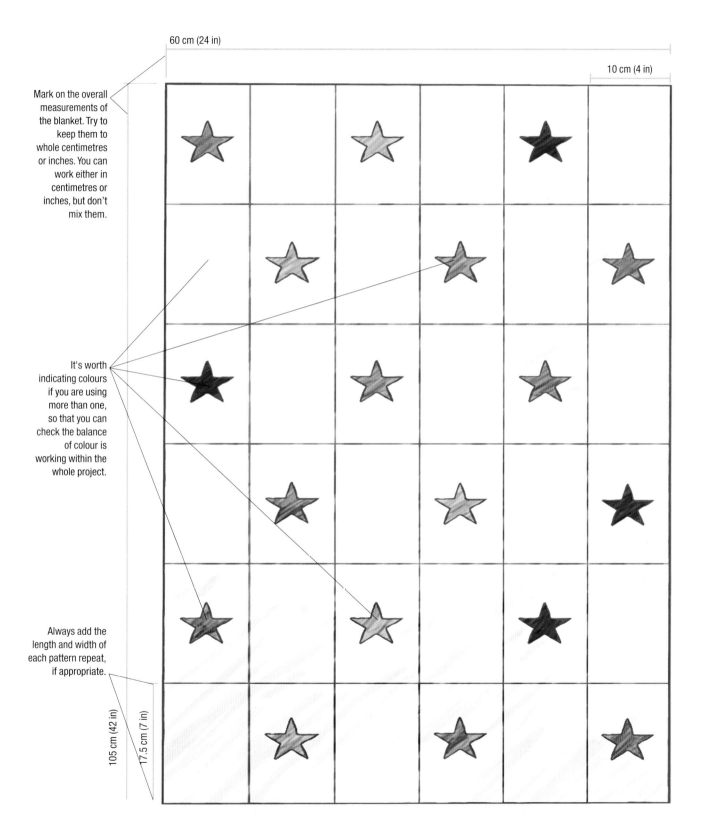

60 cm (24 in)

10 cm (4 in)

Mark on the overall measurements of the blanket. Try to keep them to whole centimetres or inches. You can work either in centimetres or inches, but don't mix them.

It's worth indicating colours if you are using more than one, so that you can check the balance of colour is working within the whole project.

Always add the length and width of each pattern repeat, if appropriate.

105 cm (42 in)

17.5 cm (7 in)

Specification drawing of a blanket with measurements written on.

Body measurements

There are points of reference on the body that can be used to help you decide on the measurements of panels for garments. Body shapes differ from person to person, so taking measurements from the person the garment is being knitted for is best for a perfect fit.

Record your own body measurements and keep them for reference. Then, when you design knitwear for yourself or you want to adapt an existing pattern to fit you, you know what all your measurements are. Do bear in mind that if you gain or lose a lot of weight, you will need to re-measure yourself.

Adding ease

Most garments will need some extra centimetres/inches added to the body measurements so that the garment fits comfortably. This is called 'ease'. The amount of ease added is determined by how loose or fitted you want the garment to be. This chart shows how much should be added to body measurements to achieve different types of fit for adult's garments.

When you have decided on the fit you want, add the required number of centimetres/inches to the body measurements. Make a note of the figures and write them on your spec drawing (see page 60).

Not too tight

Take the measurements with the tape measure fitting comfortably around the body, not pulled tight. If you are measuring yourself then ask a friend to help, as some of the measurements are quite difficult to do on your own. If you are knitting for a child, bear in mind that they grow quite quickly and it may be worth making garments a little bigger so that there is room to grow into them.

To achieve the correct fit

Type of fit	Amount to add or subtract from total
Tight fitting	subtract 1–2 cm (½–¾ in)
Close fitting	add 1–2 cm (½–¾ in)
Standard	add 3–6 cm (1¼–2¼ in)
Easy fitting	add 6–8 cm (2¼–3¼ in)
Loose fitting	add 10–15 cm (4–6 in)
Generous	add 18 cm (7 in) or more

Body measurement diagram

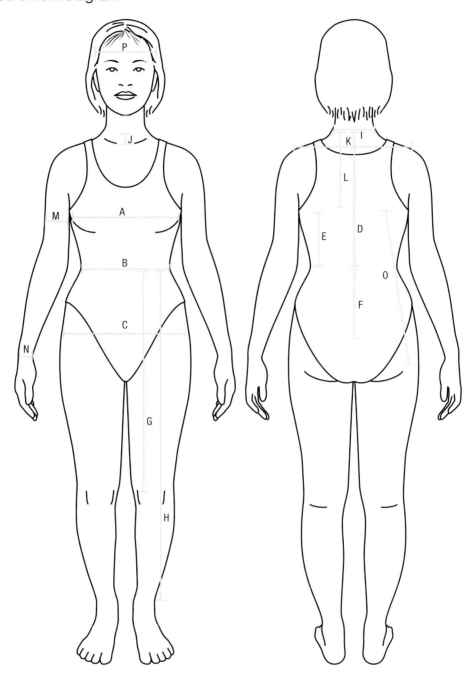

A Bust/chest measure around the widest point (this is usually about 2.5 cm (1 in) below the armhole). Make sure that the tape measure doesn't drop down across the back.

B Waist measure around the narrowest point between bust/chest and hips; this is usually in line with the navel.

C Hip measure around the widest point at the top of the thighs.

D Centre back neck to waist measure down the back of the body

E Underarm to waist remember to allow for a little extra length because when the arm is raised the garment will rise up slightly.

F Waist to hip measure down the back of the body.

G Waist to knee measure down the front of the body.

H Waist to floor measure down the front of the body.

I Back neck measure across the back of the neck.

J Front neck drop measure from the back neck line down to the collar bone.

K Shoulder to shoulder measure across the back from shoulder tip to shoulder tip.

L Armhole measure down the back of the body from the shoulder point (at neck edge) to about 5 cm (2 in) below the armpit.

M Top arm measure around the largest part of the upper arm.

N Wrist measure around the narrowest point.

O Sleeve underarm measure from armpit to wrist.

P Head circumference measure around the widest part of the head

Existing garments

If you have a garment, knitted or not, that is shaped and sized in a similar way to the one you want to design, measurements can be taken from it. Measure the garment very carefully so that you have an accurate reference to work from.

Lay the garment flat on a hard surface; a table or worktop is ideal. Measure each panel using a tape measure and making sure that you don't miss any of the small details, such as the width of the back neck, the width of the shoulders and any shaping at the armhole. Record the measurements so that they can be written on your spec drawing (see page 60).

Existing patterns

There are thousands of knitting patterns available and they can make a great starting point. Make a note of any designs you like when you are browsing through pattern books and brochures so that you build up your own pattern reference library.

You can take several different designs and amalgamate them together to create your own pattern. You might like the neckline on one garment and the sleeves on another. So look at the measurements in the pattern, compare them to your own body measurements and make amendments so that the fit and shape are as you want them.

With such a wealth of information already available, there seems little point in re-designing, for example, a raglan sleeve, if the exact shape you want already exists in a pattern that you have.

Changing yarn in a pattern

If you need to adjust the tension/gauge of an existing pattern to suit a different weight of yarn, this is quite simple to do. Firstly, you need to find out the measurements of the panels in the existing pattern.

Some of the more basic measurements, such as garment length and width, will be given in the pattern instructions and some patterns have useful schematics giving a variety of measurements. However, other details, such as the depth of an armhole shaping or the width of the shoulders, will probably not be recorded.

Read very carefully through the whole pattern and make a note of how many stitches and rows there are in each panel and in every bit of shaping. And then using the formula in Step 2 (see page 34) for calculating size from stitches and rows, you can then work out all the measurements of the existing panels. Once you have this information you can use the other formula in Step 2 (see page 44) to transpose the measurements from the existing pattern back into stitches and rows using your own tension/gauge.

Sizing charts

These charts give standard body measurements for garments. They are an ideal reference if you are unable to take measurements from the body itself. Remember that ease will have to be added to the measurements to achieve the desired fit.

You will find sizing charts for women's, men's, children's and babies' garments on pages 121–124 of this book.

Rather than starting from scratch, you can take measurements from an existing garment for your design and, if desired, translate them into a new tension/gauge for a different weight of yarn.

Measurements for accessories

Existing items, knitted or not, are the best reference for shapes and sizes for accessories. Look at your favourite accessories and imagine how gorgeous they would be knitted in a wonderful yarn.

It isn't difficult to plan a knitted accessory project: if you have a handbag that you love the shape of and want to re-create in knitting, then look at it closely to see how it has been made and measure its dimensions. Make notes of your findings, then plan out your spec drawing, using the panels of the existing bag as a guide.

After you have mapped out the basic shapes you can make alterations if you wish. For example, you may want to make the bag deeper or shallower. Do you want to add any extra details, such as a pocket or a different edge detail? Make sure you record all of the measurements on your spec drawing, including any changes you have made, so that you know the dimensions of each panel.

Do bear in mind that with knitted fabric you will not be able to precisely re-create all materials, such as a stiff leather bag that stands upright on its own, and this may affect some of your design decisions.

A favourite shopper bag would be easy to recreate in knitting.

Creating a specification drawing

When you have decided on the measurements of your knitted panels you can make a specification drawing of your design.

Using a pencil, draw out the shape of the knitted panels onto a piece of paper. You need to include every bit of shaping on your spec drawing because this is the blueprint for your design. It is a good idea to make a checklist of the measurements that you need to include on your spec drawing so that you don't forget any of them.

For example, for a round-neck sweater with a drop shoulder sleeve you should include on your list:
- Body width
- Body length (from cast-on edge to shoulder)
- Side seam length (from cast-on edge to beginning of armhole shaping)
- Shoulder width
- Back neck width
- Armhole depth
- Front neck drop
- Width of sleeve at cast-on edge
- Width of sleeve at top
- Length of sleeve

The drawing should be crisp and easy to read so that there is no confusion over the shape of the panels.

When you are happy with the drawing, re-draw the outline of each panel over the pencil marks using a pen. Then, using a pencil, write all of the measurements onto the spec drawing. If you decide to alter any of the measurements later on, the pencil can be erased and new figures can be put in.

The next step is to calculate what the measurements are in stitches and rows so that you can work out how many stitches to cast on and how many rows to knit for your design. Use the formula in Step 2 for calculating measurements (see page 44) to do this.

Seam allowances

Consider whether or not you need to add extra stitches onto the panels for seam allowances. A knitted fabric is stretchy and flexible and on loose-fitting garments, which have a lot of ease, the extra stitch may not be necessary. However, on fitted garments it is a good idea to add the extra stitch to each side edge.

Designs that have a pattern repeat on both the back and front panels will need a extra stitch at each side edge to enable the pattern to continue without a break when the panels are joined together (see page 38).

Add it up

The mathematics for both the measurements and the stitches and rows for your design must add up exactly to make the pattern work. So, slight alterations might have to be made to the calculated stitches and rows if the numbers are not tallying.

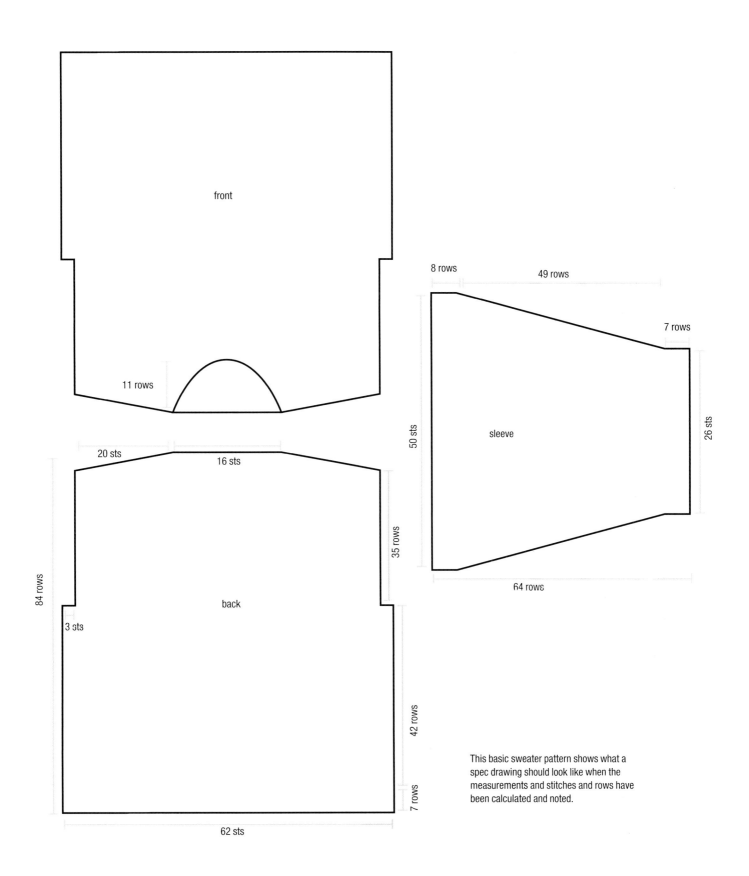

This basic sweater pattern shows what a spec drawing should look like when the measurements and stitches and rows have been calculated and noted.

Mapping out a design area on proportional graph paper

The measurements of your design are now recorded and the stitches and rows calculated. However, any shaping, such as the curve of a neckline, is given only as widths and lengths. The best way to work out these elements is to plot the stitches and rows onto proportional graph paper (see also page 32).

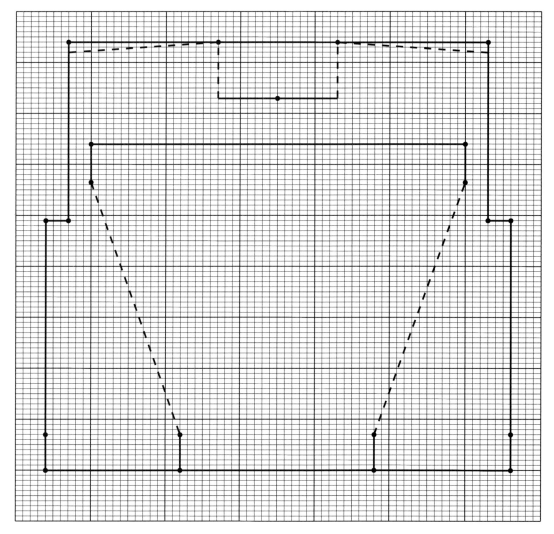

Much of this part of the design process is like doing a 'dot-to-dot' drawing. Plot out the stitches and rows you have calculated onto proportional graph paper, then join the lines together using a ruler and a pencil.

Plotting the stitches

Start by plotting out the back panel. The front panel can then be drawn on top of the back panel and the front neck shaping and any other details can be added to it later.

The width of the back neck and the depth of the front neck (referred to as the 'drop') are marked on the proportional graph paper. To draw the neckline, use a pencil (so that errors can be erased and re-drawn), to sketch a smooth curve on one side of the neck, joining the edge of the back neck to the mark for the drop of the neckline. Make sure that about one third of the central stitches across the bottom of the neckline are straight, so that the curve is smooth at the bottom rather than pointed.

The next step is to re-draw the curve to follow the lines on the proportional graph paper (see page 36). Try and stay as close as possible to the original neckline so that the curve is smooth and even. Each side of the neck will be the same shape, so it is only necessary to work out one side, and then the curve can be reversed and duplicated on the other side.

Any other curved edges, such as armholes and sleeve-heads, can be worked out on proportional graph paper in the same way.

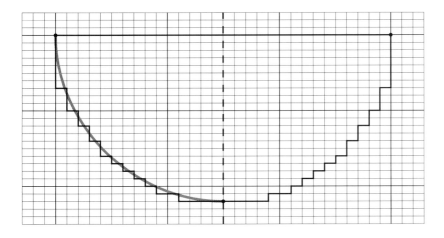

When you have drawn the neckline on both sides you can use the graph to work out on which rows you need to decrease stitches to create the neck shaping.

Shaping

Shaped, slanted sections of a design can also be drawn as lines on proportional graph paper and squared off, or a mathematical calculation can be used to work out where to increase or decrease stitches. Using the sleeve panel for the basic sweater (see page 67) as an example, this is how you work out the shaping mathematically.

Increases

Firstly, note that the cuff is worked straight, then the sleeve is shaped by increasing stitches along each side until it is the desired width. The increases must be planned at regular intervals so that the diagonal slant is smooth. To keep the sleeve symmetrical, the increases must also be paired – in other words, there must be one increase at each end of every increase row.

To create a neat shape that will fit comfortably into the armhole there should be at least 2.5 cm (1 in) of straight knitting at the top of the sleeve between the last increase and the cast/bind-off edge.

Half the work

It is not always necessary to draw out the whole pattern for the front, back and sleeves. Instead, you can save time and space on the proportional graph paper by imagining a fold line down the middle of the panels and drawing out only half of each one. This works for designs that are symmetrical, but will not work for asymmetric panels.

Before turning to the formula below, you need to know the following:
- The number of stitches at the bottom of the sleeve, after the cuff (narrowest point).
- The number of stitches at the top (widest point) of the sleeve.
- The number of rows for the sleeve (minus the cuff and 2.5 cm (1 in) at the top of the sleeve).

Calculating increases along a diagonal edge

- Subtract the number of stitches at the bottom of the sleeve from the number of stitches at the top, then divide this figure by two (for paired increases).
- Divide the number of rows for the sleeve by the number of paired increases to give you the number of rows between increases.
- Ignore numbers beyond the decimal point, if there are any. Take the whole number before the decimal point as the number of rows between increases and work the remaining rows straight before working the final 2.5 cm (1 in) straight.

Worked example: sleeve increases

Study this example of sleeve increases for the basic sweater (see page 67) to help you put this formula into practice in your own designs.

100 stitches (top of sleeve) minus 50 stitches (bottom of sleeve) = 50 stitches
50 stitches divided by 2 = 25 pairs of increases
122 rows (sleeve length) divided by 25 = 4.88, which must be rounded to the whole number before the decimal point, so 4.

Therefore, the pattern will read as follows:
Increase 1 stitch either side every 4th row to 100 stitches (which is 100 rows) and work the remaining 22 rows straight. Work another 2.5 cm (1 in) straight. Cast/bind off.

If the number of rows to be worked straight at the top of the sleeve is more than you would like, then you can alter the shaping.

If you increase 1 stitch either side every 4th row to 100 stitches (which is 100 rows) there will be 22 rows remaining.

The 22 remaining rows can be incorporated into the shaping by increasing every 5th row for 22 of the 25 increases.

On this type of sleeve the increases should be more frequent at the bottom than at the top so therefore the pattern will read as follows:
Increase 1 stitch either side every 4th row 3 times and then every following 5th row 22 times to 122 stitches (which is 100 rows). Work another 2.5 cm (1 in) straight. Cast/bind off.

Decreases

The principle and formula for working out decreases is exactly the same as those for increases, just substitute the word 'decrease' for 'increase' throughout.

These two formulas can be used to work out the increases and decreases for any diagonally shaped edges on your design.

The regular decreasing along the edges of this armhole and sleeve meet up perfectly to give a fully-fashioned look to the sweater.

Fully fashioning

It is a good idea to place increases and decreases at least one stitch in from the edge of your knitting. If increases and decreases are made on the very edges of the knitting, the edges become irregular in shape and are consequently very tricky to seam together. When you increase and decrease stitches a small fashioning mark is created where the stitches have been knitted together or increased, and this can look very effective if the shapings are placed a few stitches in from the edge of the work. This is called fully fashioning and is usually associated with more expensive knitwear.

This is an example of how you could fully fashion a garment knitted in stocking/stockinette stitch:

- On increase rows: (RS): K3, make 1 stitch, knit to last 3 stitches, make 1 stitch, K3.
- On decrease rows: (RS): K3, K2tog, knit to last 3 sts, K2togtbl, K3.

Deciding which way to knit

Before you draft your final design you must decide how you are going to knit the panels. The conventional way to knit an accessory or garment is to work from bottom to top, but there are other ways to knit.

Side-to-side

This method turns the knitting on its side and uses stitches to determine length and rows to determine width. If you use this method there are several things to bear in mind when you are planning out the design.

Welts (see page 38) will have to be added onto the panels after they have been completed, either by picking up stitches or by knitting the welts separately and sewing them on.

On a garment, the front neck shaping (especially if it is curved rather than square) will be a bit trickier to knit and can look a bit untidy. However, it will make patterns such as vertical stripes much easier to knit, because they will in fact be knitted horizontally.

When you are planning a side-to-side garment on proportional graph paper, remember to turn the paper on its side (see page 32).

Basic shapes

On pages 82–114 you will find directions and advice on designing and knitting a range of accessories and garments. And at the back of the book are pages of proportional graph paper for you to map out your designs on.

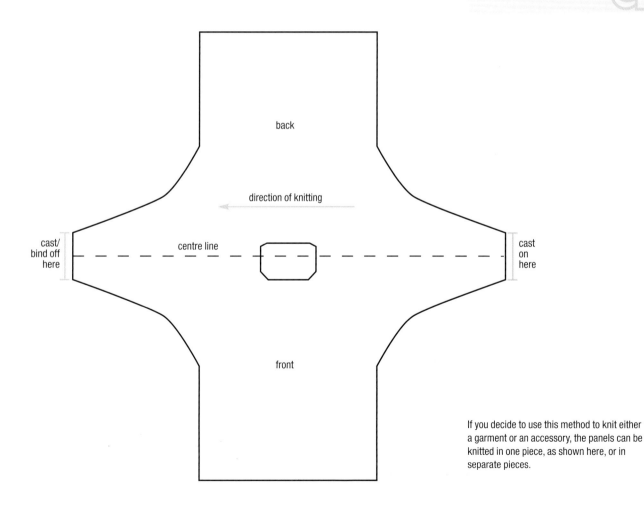

back

direction of knitting

cast/
bind off
here

centre line

cast
on
here

front

If you decide to use this method to knit either a garment or an accessory, the panels can be knitted in one piece, as shown here, or in separate pieces.

In one piece

If you use this method to knit a garment, then the front and back panels and the sleeves can all be worked in one piece, which eliminates shoulder and armhole seams. It is a good way to work if you want patterns to run continuously and in the same direction across the panels.

You will start knitting at the bottom of the front panel, a divide will need to be made for the neck opening at the appropriate point, the neck will be shaped (see pages 115–117) and then the stitches will have to be cast back on again to close the back neck.

Any shaping, such as the underarm on the sleeve, will have to be created by casting on and casting off sets of stitches at calculated intervals rather than increasing stitches in the conventional way.

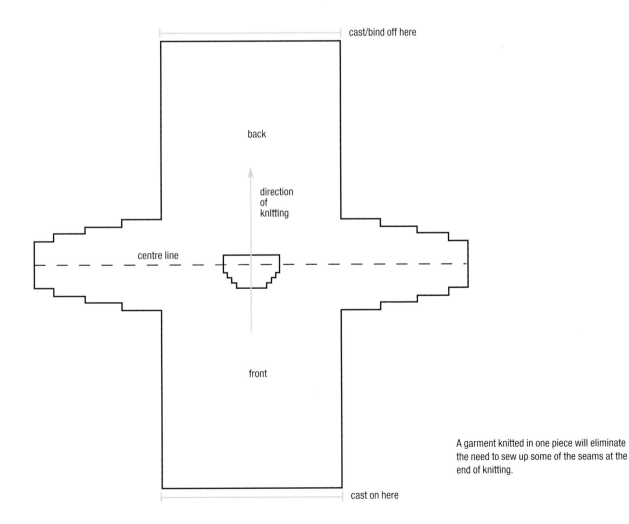

cast/bind off here

back

direction of knitting

centre line

front

cast on here

A garment knitted in one piece will eliminate the need to sew up some of the seams at the end of knitting.

From the centre out

This method is ideal for using up oddments of yarn and can help you create knitted panels that have vertical, symmetrical patterns across them. Each panel is knitted side-to-side, rather than bottom to top.

You start to knit the panel in the centre, using a provisional cast-on to begin the first half (this will make the join in the centre invisible), and work across to the side edge. When the half-panel is completed the stitches can be picked up along the provisional cast-on and the knitting can be worked back the other way, duplicating the pattern and stitches of the first half.

If you have a limited quantity of different yarns that you are going to use for the project and you are worried that you might run out of some of them, you can ensure that a symmetrical pattern will be created by working both halves of the panel simultaneously.

If you are working on a garment, the stitches for the sleeves can be picked up when both the back and front panels are completed and knitted down to the cuff.

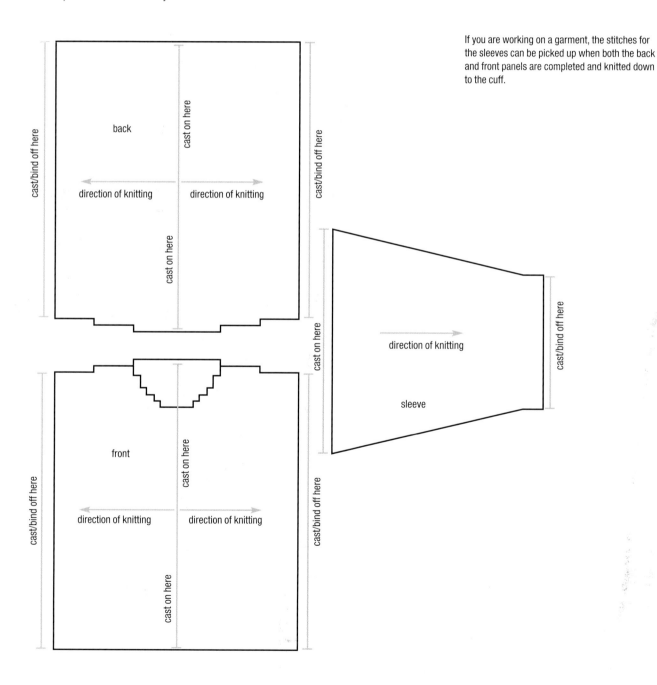

Start by working a few rows of the first half and then put these stitches on a holder. Next, make a start on the second half and work the same number of rows as the first half, in the same pattern. Then work back and forth between the two halves of the panel, working a few rows at a time until the whole panel is completed.

Circular (in the round)

This is the preferred method for many knitters because it eliminates the side seams. A conventional pattern (knitted from bottom to top) is quite easy to convert to circular because the panels are usually worked in the same direction. However, the side 'seams' must be marked so that you know where the beginning and end of a round is. It is worth noting that the omission of side seams will mean that the project has less structure. Consequently a softer and more casual shape will be created, which means that this is not the best method if you want a fitted, tailored look.

Any shaping in the panels, increases and decreases, should be knitted either side of a marked stitch to ensure that they are symmetrical and in the correct place. On a garment, the stitches will have to be transferred onto straight needles when the armhole begins, unless you are knitting with steeks.

If your tension/gauge across stocking/stockinette stitch is usually a little uneven, knitting in the round will help sort this out because you only ever work right-side (knit) rows.

Changes to patterns

Knitting in the round eliminates working any wrong side rows because you knit continuously round in a circle in one direction and all of the most common stitches like garter, moss/seed stitch and rib can still be worked. However, it should be remembered that to create a stitch like garter stitch, some changes will have to be made to the pattern. For example, on straight needles garter stitch is created by knitting all stitches on both wrong side and right side rows. But when you work in the round garter stitch is created by knitting and purling alternate rounds. And if you are knitting a rib in the round you will have to knit where you knitted and purl where you purled on all rows to keep the pattern correct.

STEP 5 GETTING KNITTING

Calculating yarn quantities

Before you start knitting your project you need to work out how much yarn to buy so that you have everything ready. Then you can confidently start knitting without fear of running out of yarn.

Simplifying your spec drawing

The first step towards calculating yarn quantities is to simplify the project panels on your specification drawing (see page 66) to make them into basic rectangles. In these examples we are using a basic sweater pattern. Turn the back, front and sleeve panels into rectangles by drawing a coloured line around each panel at the widest and longest points.

When calculating how much yarn you need it is not necessary to add on any extra for features such as collars, neckbands or pockets, unless they are extraordinarily large. Simplifying the back, front and sleeve panels as illustrated should allow for enough yarn to make these details. However, yarn calculations are approximate, so it is always wise to buy an extra ball of each colour yarn to avoid disappointment.

Calculating yarn for a one-colour project

• Work out the area of each rectangular panel on your spec drawing (width multiplied by length = area in cm (in) squared).
• Add the areas of all of the panels together.
• Divide the total area of the panels by the area of the swatch (in other words, work out how many times your swatch will fit into the area of the panels).
• Multiply this figure by the weight of the swatch to give the quantity of yarn needed for your project.

The quantity of yarn for a one-colour sweater is easy to calculate.

Worked example: calculating yarn for a one-colour sweater

This example shows you how to put the formula into practice.
The swatch measures 10 x 10 cm (4 x 4 in), so its area is 100 cm (16 in) squared.
The weight of the swatch is 15 g (½ oz).

Front and back (both the same)	56 cm (22 in) multiplied by 60 cm (24 in) = 3360 cm (528 in) squared (each panel). Total area of back and front panels is 3360 cm (528 in) multiplied by 2 = 6720 cm (1056 in) squared.
Sleeves (both the same) swatch area	50 cm (20 in) multiplied by 49 cm (19 in) = 2450 cm (380 in) squared. Total area of both sleeves is 2450 cm (380 in) multiplied by 2 = 4900 cm (760 in) squared.
Total area of all panels	6720 (1056) plus 4900 (760) = 11620 cm (1816 in) squared.
Divide panel area by	11620 cm (1816 in) squared (total area of the panels) divided by 100 cm (16 in) squared (area of swatch) = 116.2 (113.5)
Multiply by swatch weight	116.2 (113.5) multiplied by 15 g (½ oz) = 1743 g (57 oz). Therefore, it will take approximately 1.75 kg (3½ lb) of yarn to knit the sweater.

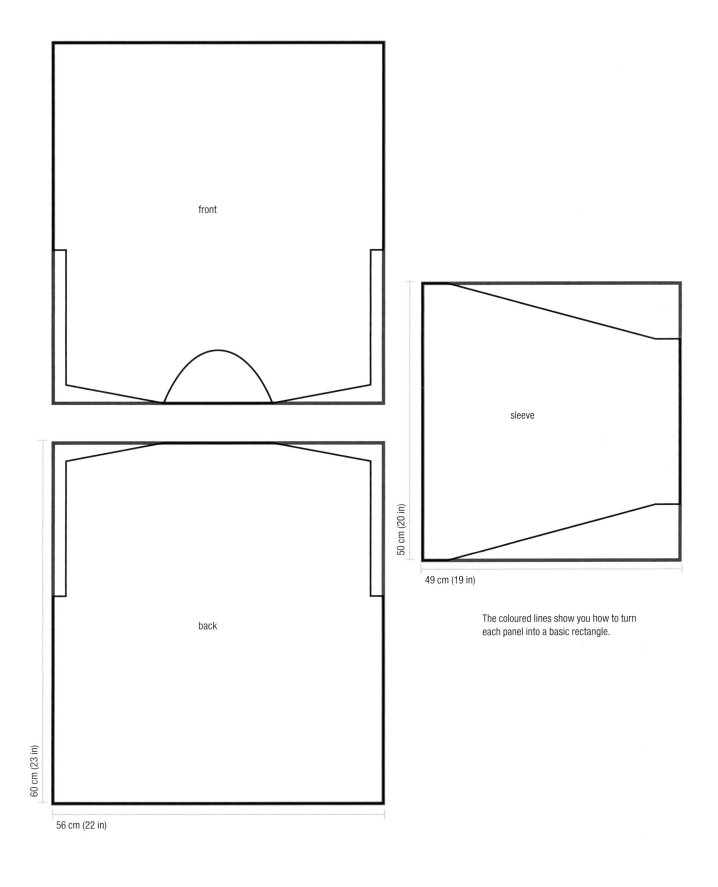

front

back

sleeve

60 cm (23 in)

56 cm (22 in)

50 cm (20 in)

49 cm (19 in)

The coloured lines show you how to turn
each panel into a basic rectangle.

Multi-coloured projects

To calculate how much yarn of each colour to buy, you will need to know the weight to the nearest gram/ounce of each ball of yarn before and after you knitted your swatch (see page 55). You will also need to know the area of your swatch.

The calculation for a multi-coloured project is worked out using the same formula as for a one-colour project, but first you need to work out how much of each colour was used in the swatch. To do this, subtract the weight of each ball after knitting the swatch from its weight before starting.

Getting it right

Your swatch should reflect as precisely as possible the proportion of each colour used in your design so that you can make an accurate calculation of the quantity needed of each yarn.

Worked example: calculating yarns for a multi-colour sweater

This example uses the same sweater as before, but in three colours.
The swatch measures 10 x 10 cm (4 x 4 in), so its area is 100 cm (16 in) squared.
The weight of the swatch is 15 g (½ oz).
The weights of the three colours used in the swatch are:

Red	6 g (0.2 oz)
Blue	4 g (0.14 oz)
Yellow	5 g (0.18 oz)
Percentages of the colours used in the swatch	100 (per cent) divided by 15 g (0.5 oz) (total weight of swatch) = 6.66 (200)
Red	6 g (0.2 oz) multiplied by 6.66 (200) = 39.9 (40), which has to be rounded to a whole number, so 40%.
Blue	4 g (0.14 oz) multiplied by 6.66 (200) = 26.6 (28), which has to be rounded to a whole number, so 27%.
Yellow	5 g (0.18 oz) multiplied by 6.66 (200) = 33.3 (36), which has to be rounded to a whole number, so 33%. Therefore, around 40% of the swatch is red, 27% is blue and 33% is yellow. After the calculation has been made for the quantity of yarn (the same as for the one-colour sweater), we know that the total amount of yarn required for the project is 1743 g (55 oz).
How much of each colour is required?	1743 g (55 oz) (total weight of yarn needed) divided by 100% = 17.43 (0.55).
Red	17.43 (0.55) multiplied by 40% = 697.2 (22), which has to be rounded to a whole number, so 697 g (22 oz).
Blue	17.43 (0.55) multiplied by 27% = 470.6 (14.85), which has to be rounded to a whole number, so 471 g (15 oz).
Yellow	17.43 (0.55) multiplied by 33% = 575.1 (18.15), which has to be rounded to a whole number, so 575 g (18 oz). Therefore, it will take approximately 675 g (22 oz) of red, 475 g (15 oz) of blue and 575 g (18 oz) of yellow yarn to knit the sweater.

Writing up patterns

Write up your pattern before you start knitting so that you have clear instructions to work from. This is especially important if you are going to give the project to another knitter to make. If you have worked out your design on proportional graph paper (see page 68), you will need to 'read' the pattern from this.

Once you have established your own style of writing a pattern, use it for every project that you design so that you become confident in your patterns. If other knitters are knitting up your designs they will soon become familiar with your style and find your patterns easier to read.

Elements to consider when writing a pattern

• At the beginning of the instructions give the finished size of the project and list the materials needed (yarn, needles and any embellishments).
• State the tension/gauge, including what it is to be measured over (stocking/stockinette stitch or the pattern), and the recommended needle size to use (see page 57).
• Decide whether to write the pattern in centimetres or inches.
• Decide whether to refer to the needles in metric or US sizes (a needle conversion table is on page 125).
• On page 125 you will find a list of standard abbreviations that you can use throughout the pattern; this will shorten its length and means less writing!
• Indicate any change of needle size (for example, after the welt).
• Make sure that any shaping is clearly written out so that the knitter knows exactly on which row to increase/decrease.
• Indicate which technique should be used if there is any colour work in the design (intarsia, Fair Isle, or both).
• Include a key for a chart (if you have one), so that it is clear what the different symbols mean.
• Give basic instructions for assembling the panels.

Favourite pattern style

If you have a favourite brand of knitting pattern that you find especially easy to follow, why not base your pattern writing on this, using the existing patterns as a guide?

Basic shapes

The next step is to plan out your spec drawing with all of the measurements written onto it and then work out how the panels for your project are going to be knitted and assembled together.

The following instructions and diagrams show you how to construct various accessories and garments. All of them are basic shapes that are a starting point for a knitting project and that can be adapted and experimented with if you want to develop them further.

To avoid complication, all of the panels are worked in the conventional method, which is knitted from bottom to top, except for the hat and socks which are traditionally worked in the round (see page 75). All of the projects are knitted in stocking/stockinette stitch unless stated otherwise.

Throughout this section you will be told to calculate the numbers of stitches and rows needed for specific panels; always use the formula on page 44 to do this.

Scarf

How to design and knit a scarf

1 Calculate the number of stitches you need to cast on for the width of the scarf (A).
2 Calculate the number of rows you need to knit for the length of the scarf (B).
3 Cast/bind off stitches (C).

Points to consider for scarves

- You can make the scarf as long and as wide as you like.
- Use a soft, non-scratchy yarn that is comfortable against the skin.
- Make sure that the fabric quality is soft and fluid (see page 57) so that the scarf can be wrapped and tied easily around the neck.
- A scarf is double-sided, so knit it in a stitch or pattern that looks good on both sides.
- A welt in a firm stitch, such as rib, moss/seed or garter (see pages 38–39), could be knitted at each end of the scarf to stabilize it and stop it from curling (A and C).
- Both sides of the scarf (B) are finished edges so they must be knitted neatly. You can create a neat edge, or 'selvedge', by knitting the first and last stitch of every row or slipping the first stitch at the beginning of every row.
- To stop the edges (B) from curling, a narrow border could be knitted in a firm stitch.
- To finish the edges (A and C), pompoms, tassels or a fringe could be added to the scarf after it has been cast/bind off. These should be factored in when buying the yarn.

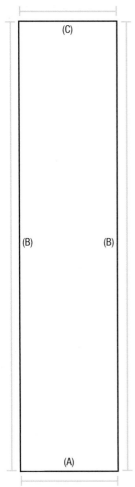

Blanket knitted in separate squares

How to design and knit a blanket

1 Decide on the size of each individual square and calculate the number of stitches and rows you need to knit one square.

2 Work out how many squares you need to knit to achieve the size of the blanket (in other words, work out how many squares fit into the design area).

3 Plan out the order of piecing so that you know how many of each square to knit.

How to join the panels

4 Using mattress stitch, sew the squares together in the correct order to create the blanket.

Points to consider for blankets

- Any type of yarn can be used to knit a blanket, but remember that cotton or cotton mixes will create a heavier blanket than wool or acrylic yarns.

- Make sure that all of the squares knit up to the same size so that they piece together easily.

- The finished size of the blanket might have to be compromised slightly depending on the size of the individual squares.

- Knit the squares to a firm tension/gauge rather than a loose one to help stop the blanket stretching or dropping.

- When the squares are joined, a stitch at each side of each square will be taken into a seam and this could reduce the width of the finished blanket by quite a few centimetres/inches.

- When all of the squares are sewn together, finish the blanket with a knitted border by either picking up stitches around all four edges or knitting a separate border and sewing it on. If stitches are picked up it is best to pick up each edge individually and mitre the ends so that the borders can be joined neatly at each corner.

- The finished blanket can be lined using either a woven or jersey fabric and this will cover up the seams and any untidiness on the wrong side of the work. It will also stabilize the shape of the blanket and stop it from stretching.

Sew simple

To make sewing up the blanket easier, the squares could be knitted in vertical strips (A, B, C, D and E) and then the strips could be sewn together, eliminating any horizontal seams. When working a strip, cast/bind off the stitches at the top of each square and then pick up the stitches along the cast/bind-off edge to begin the next square.

The border for the blanket should be knitted in a firm stitch, such as garter stitch which will stabilize the edges of the finished piece.

(A)   (B)   (C)   (D)   (E)

Cushion with a flap and button fastening

How to design and knit a cushion

1 Calculate the number of stitches you need to cast on for the width of the front panel (A).

2 Calculate the number of rows you need to knit for the length of the front panel (B).

3 Cast/bind off stitches (C).

4 Knit the back panel to match the front panel, casting on at (D) and casting off at (F).

5 Knit the cushion flap to match the width of the front panel (G to match C).

6 Calculate the number of rows you need to knit for the length of the cushion flap (H).

7 Plan out evenly spaced buttonholes along the edge of the cushion flap (as indicated on the spec), before working a few more rows and casting off the stitches (J).

How to join the panels

8 Sew the cast-on edge of the front panel to the cast-on edge of the back panel (A to D).

9 Sew the cast/bind-off edge of the front panel to the cast-on edge of the cushion flap (C to G).

10 Sew the side edges of the front and back panels together (B to E).

11 Sew on buttons to align with the buttonholes in the flap.

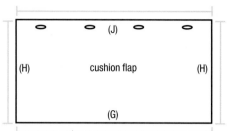

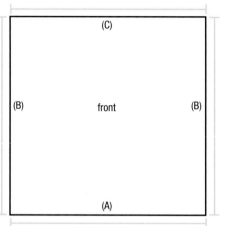

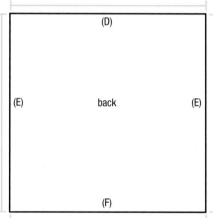

This is the simplest construction for a cushion cover and is very easy to knit.

Cushion with a horizontal centre-back button fastening

How to design and knit a cushion

1. Calculate the number of stitches you need to cast on for the width of the front panel (K).
2. Calculate the number of rows you need to knit for the length of the front panel (L).
3. Cast/bind off stitches (M).
4. Knit the upper back panel to match the width of the front panel (N to match M).
5. Calculate the number of rows you need to knit for the length of the upper back panel (P), making sure that it is exactly half the length of the front panel.
6. Plan out evenly spaced buttonholes along the next row of the upper back panel (as indicated on the spec), before working a few more rows and casting off the stitches (Q).
7. Knit the lower back panel to match the width of the front panel (R to match K).
8. Knit the lower back panel until it is approximately 5 cm (2 in) longer (S) than the upper back panel.
9. Cast/bind off stitches (T).

How to join the panels

10. Sew the cast/bind-off edge of the front panel to the cast-on edge of the upper back panel (M to N).
11. Sew the cast-on edge of the front panel to the cast-on edge of the lower back panel (K to R).
12. Sew the side edges of the front panel to the side edges of the upper back panel (L to P), making sure that the buttonholes align with the centre point of the front panel on both sides.
13. Sew the side edges of the front panel to the side edges of the lower back panel (L to S), inserting the cast/bind-off edge of the lower back panel (T) under the cast/bind-off edge of the upper back panel (Q).
14. Sew on buttons to align with the buttonholes.

Points to consider for both cushions

- Check what size cushion pads are available in the shops before you decide on the size of your cushion cover. If the pad size you want is not available to buy you will have to make one yourself.
- Knit the panels to a firm tension/gauge so that the finished cushion cover does not stretch too much when the pad is inserted, otherwise the pad could show through the knitted fabric.
- The panels could be knitted by picking up stitches along the cast-on and cast/bind-off edges if preferred, rather than knitting separate panels and sewing them together.
- The seams at the side edges and along the cast-on and cast/bind-off edges of the front panel will give the finished cushion cover strength and shape. But if a softer shape is preferred the cover could be knitted in one piece with seams along the side edges only.
- It is a good idea to knit a welt in a firm stitch, such as rib, moss/seed or garter (see pages 16–18), along all of the finished edges (F, J, Q and T) before casting off stitches. This will stabilize the edges and stop them from curling.
- Make sure that there are enough rows in the welts on the cushion flap and the upper back panel to accommodate the buttonholes. They need to be positioned across the middle of the welt with an equal number of rows before and after the buttonholes before casting off.

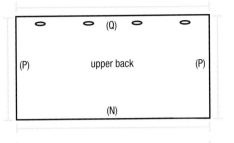

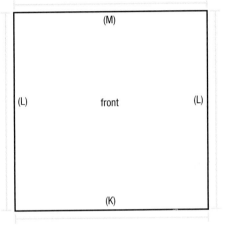

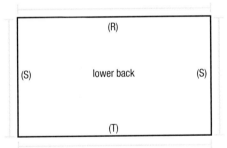

This type of cushion construction uses less yarn than the cushion with a flap and button fastening.

Drawstring bag

How to design and knit a drawstring bag

1 Calculate the number of stitches you need to cast on for the width of the front panel (A).

2 Calculate the number of rows you need to knit for the length of the front panel (B) up to the beginning of the hem (C).

3 Knit a small eyelet at each side of the panel a few rows after casting on and a few stitches in from the edges (for the drawstrings to be threaded through).

4 Calculate the number of rows you need to knit for the depth of the hem (C), making sure that it is deep enough for the drawstrings to pass through it twice. A knitted fold line (as indicated on the spec) will help the hem fold over easily.

5 Cast/bind off stitches (D).

6 Knit the back panel to match the front panel (including the eyelets and hem), casting on at (E) and casting off at (H).

How to join the panels

7 Sew the cast-on edge of the front panel to the cast-on edge of the back panel (A to E).

8 Sew the side edges of the back and front panels together (B to F), stopping at the beginning of the hems.

9 Following the instructions for how to thread the drawstrings, below, place drawstrings inside the hems on the front and back panels,

10 Close both of the hems by folding them in half and slip-stitching them down on the inside of the bag.

How to thread the drawstrings

11 Lay the bag on a flat surface with the front panel face up.

12 Thread one end of the drawstring from back to front through the eyelet on the left-hand side.

13 Lay the drawstring along the length of the left-hand side seam, then inside the hem at the top of the front panel, pinning the hem down in place as you lay the drawstring across.

14 Continue to lay the drawstring inside the hem at the top of the back panel, pinning as before, and then take it back down the length of the left-hand side seam.

15 Thread the end of the drawstring front to back through the same eyelet on the left-hand side.

16 Fasten the drawstring by knotting the two ends together.

17 Repeat steps 11–16 with the second drawstring, but take it through the eyelets on the right-hand side and up the right-hand side seam instead of the left.

18 The hem that has been pinned down can be unpinned and then pinned again into place after the second drawstring has been threaded through.

Points to consider for drawstring bags

• Knit the panels to a firm tension/gauge so that the bag holds its shape when it has items inside it.

• The panels could be knitted by picking up stitches along the cast-on edge if preferred, rather than knitting separate panels and sewing them together.

• After knitting the fold line across the hem, knit the second part of the hem on a slightly smaller needle so that when it is folded back and sewn down, it will fit neatly inside the bag.

• The drawstrings could be either knitted cords, or they could be bought ribbon, leather thongs or cord.

• The bag could be lined. The lining should be cut so that it sits slightly short of the bottom of the bag and then the knitting will not stretch when items are placed in it.

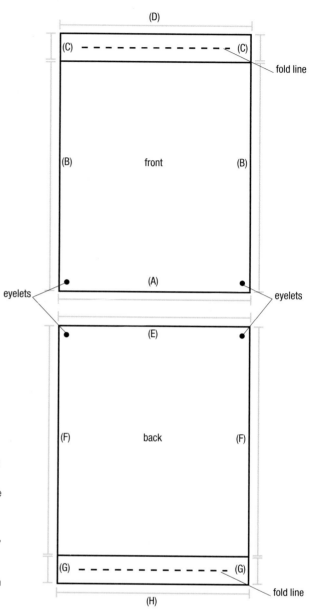

This casual bag shape is ideal for both kids and adults alike to use, and has a soft, rounded shape.

Bag with base and side gussets

How to design and knit a bag with base and side gussets

1 Calculate the number of stitches you need to cast on for the width of the base panel (A).

2 Calculate the number of rows you need to knit for the depth of the base panel (B).

3 Cast/bind off stitches (C).

4 Knit the front panel to match the width of the base panel (D to match A/C).

5 Calculate the number of rows you need to knit for the length of the front panel (E).

6 Cast/bind off stitches (F).

7 Knit the back panel to match the front panel, casting on at (G) and casting off at (J).

8 Knit two side gussets to match the depth of the base panel (width of K to match depth of B), and the length of the front and back panels (L to match E/H), casting on at K and casting off at M.

9 Knit a strap to the desired length.

How to join the panels

10 Sew the cast/bind-off edge of the base panel to the cast-on edge of the front panel (C to D).

11 Sew the cast-on edge of the base panel to the cast-on edge of the back panel (A to G).

12 Sew side gussets to base panel (K to B).

13 Sew front and back panels to side gussets (L to E and L to H).

14 Sew each end of the strap in place at the top of the side gussets (M).

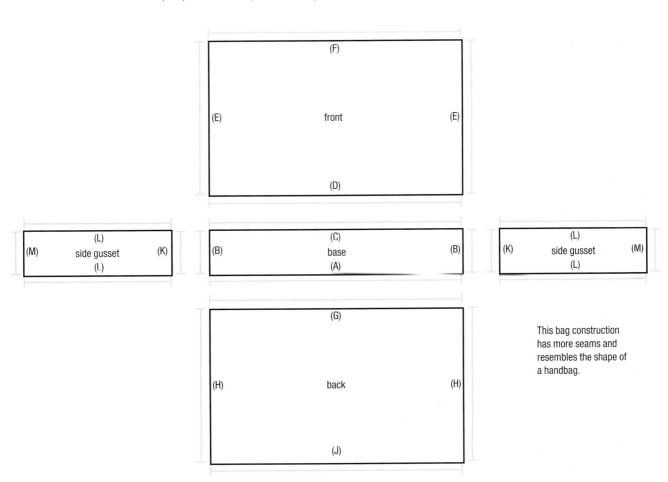

This bag construction has more seams and resembles the shape of a handbag.

Points to consider for bags with base and side gussets

- Knit the base panel in a firm stitch, such as rib, moss/seed or garter (see pages 16–18), and use a smaller needle than is used for the front and back panels to ensure a tight tension/gauge.

- The panels could be knitted by picking up stitches along the cast-on and cast/bind-off edges if preferred, rather than knitting separate panels and sewing them together.

- Knit the front and back panels to a firm tension/gauge so that the bag keeps its shape when items are inside it.

- The side gussets could be tapered towards the top by decreasing a few stitches between (K) and (M) to give a better shape to the bag.

- It is a good idea to knit a welt in a firm stitch, such as rib, moss/seed or garter (see pages 16–18), along all of the finished edges (F, J and M) before casting off the stitches. This will stabilize the edges and stop them from curling.

- The strap should be knitted to a tight tension/gauge and in a firm stitch so that it has limited elasticity. A piece of woven fabric could be sewn to the underside of the strap to stop it from stretching.

- The bag will probably need some kind of fastening to stop it from gaping open at the top. This could be a button, press-stud, Velcro, a zip or a drawstring. This should be planned out before you start knitting so that you include the fastening and any details such as buttonholes or eyelets in the design.

- The bag could be lined. The lining should be cut so that it sits slightly short of the bottom of the bag and then the knitting will not stretch when items are placed in it.

Stripe patterns look great on knitted hats and are easy to knit.

Hat

How to design and knit a hat

This is knitted on circular and double-pointed needles.

1 Calculate the number of stitches you need for the circumference of the hat (A). Make sure that the knitted circumference is approximately 5 cm (2 in) shorter than the measurement of the circumference around the head to achieve a snug fit.

2 Calculate the number of rounds you need to knit for the depth of the hat (B).

3 Calculate the number of rounds you need to knit without any shaping up to the beginning of the crown (D). (The crown is indicated by a dotted line on the spec and usually measures 8–10 cm (3¼–4 in) for an adult or a child.)

4 The number of rounds up to the beginning of the crown (D), subtracted from the number of rounds for the depth of the hat (B) will give you the number of rounds for the crown.

5 At the top of the crown (C), there should be approximately 2.5 cm (1 in) of stitches left after the decreasing has been completed. Calculate the number of stitches at the top of the crown (C) and subtract it from the number of stitches calculated for the circumference of the hat (A). This gives you the amount of stitches that need to be decreased around the crown.

6 Work out an even distribution of the decreases across the number of rounds calculated for the depth of the crown. At the same time, you need to decide how many decreases are going to be made across a round and where the decreases are going to be worked. The decreases should be shaped gradually, spacing them closer together towards the top of the crown. This will help to create a smooth curve around the top of the hat. Planning the decreases for the crown might be easier to work out on proportional graph paper or on a diagram.

Points to consider for hats

- It is a good idea to knit a welt in a firm stitch, such as rib, moss/seed or garter (see pages 16–18), at the beginning of the hat for at least 2.5 cm (1 in) to stabilize the edge.

- If the hat has a turn-back cuff, the hat should be knitted to the same circumference as the head measurement.

- Begin knitting the hat on a circular needle (which must be shorter than the circumference of the stitches), and then change to four or five double-pointed needles to shape the crown.

- Use markers to mark the beginning of a round and where the decreases are going to be made for the crown so that they are worked in the same place on every round.

- Pompoms or tassels could be sewn to the top of the crown after the hat has been completed. These must be factored in when buying the yarn.

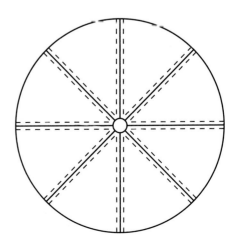

The crown, looking down from above. Double decreases (indicated by dashes), are made at each decrease point.

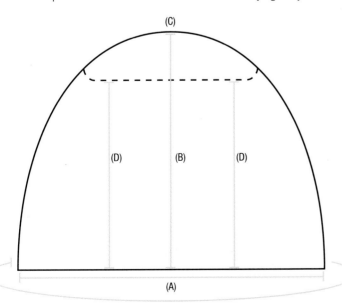

knitted in the round

Socks

How to design and knit a sock

The sock is knitted on a set of four double-pointed needles, beginning at the calf and finishing at the toe.

1 Calculate the number of stitches that you need to cast on for the width at the top of the sock (A), rounding it up or down if necessary to make an even number. If possible, cast on a number of stitches that are divisible by 3 as this will help the dividing up of the stitches onto double-pointed needles.

2 Calculate the number of rounds you need to knit for the height of the sock (C).

3 Divide the stitches evenly onto a set of four double-pointed needles (put the stitches on three needles and use the fourth needle to knit with), and knit to the beginning of the heel flap.

4 For the heel flap, divide the total number of stitches for the sock in half and put one half on one needle (referred to as needle 1). If this doesn't give you an odd number of stitches, slip one stitch onto one of the other needles to give you an odd number of stitches on needle 1. This odd stitch is the 'guide' stitch, which is the centre stitch of the heel flap and it should be marked so that it can be easily identified. Leave the remaining stitches on the other two needles (these are the stitches for the instep). Continue to knit straight (back and forth) on the heel flap stitches only, until the flap fits around the curve of the heel (this is approximately 6 cm (2¼ in) for a man, 5 cm (2 in) for a woman and 4 cm (1½ in) or less for a child), finishing on a wrong-side row (right-side facing for next row).

5 Turning the heel:

Right side Knit to 2 stitches past the centre stitch, slip 1 stitch, knit 1 stitch, pass the slipped stitch over the knit stitch, knit 1 stitch, turn the work.

Wrong side Slip 1 stitch, purl to 2 stitches past the centre stitch, purl 2 stitches together, purl 1 stitch, turn the work.

Right side Slip 1 stitch, knit to 3 stitches past the centre stitch, slip 1 stitch, knit 1 stitch, pass the slipped stitch over the knit stitch, knit 1 stitch, turn the work.

Wrong side Slip 1 stitch, purl to 3 stitches past the centre stitch, purl 2 stitches together, purl 1 stitch, turn the work.

Continue to turn the heel in this way, adding one extra stitch to those worked past the centre stitch on each pair of right-side and wrong-side rows, until all of the stitches have been used, ending with a wrong side row. With the right side of the work facing towards you, knit to the centre stitch of the heel.

6 For the instep shaping, knit the remaining stitches for the heel flap, then pick up stitches along the side of the heel flap. Make sure that the stitches are picked up evenly (this will mean picking up less stitches than there are rows, see page 116).

7 Using a second needle (referred to as needle 2), knit across the stitches that have been left on the other two needles (these are the instep stitches).

8 Using a third needle (referred to as needle 3), pick up stitches along the other side of the heel flap (to match the first side of the heel), and then knit to the centre stitch of the heel flap. The stitches are now joined again in the round.

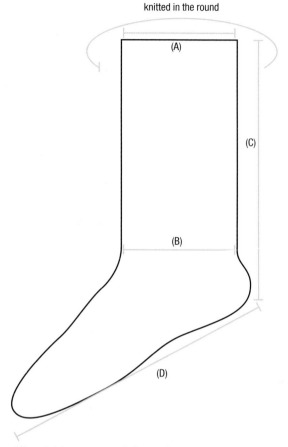

knitted in the round

Where to take measurements for a sock.
Calf At the desired height of the sock (A).
Ankle This is the same width as the foot (B).
Length of sock From the centre back of the heel up to the sock top (C).
Length of foot From the bottom of the heel to the longest point of the toes (D).

Shaping the instep on three needles.

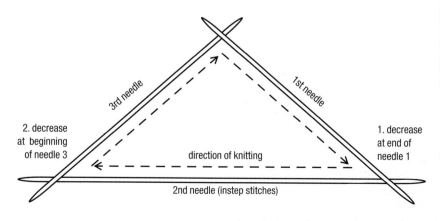

3rd needle

1st needle

2. decrease at beginning of needle 3

direction of knitting

1. decrease at end of needle 1

2nd needle (instep stitches)

9 The instep is shaped by decreasing stitches at the end of needle 1 and at the beginning of needle 3, as follows: work until there are three stitches left on needle 1, knit two stitches together, knit 1 stitch. Knit across the instep stitches (on needle 2). At the beginning of needle 3, knit 1 stitch, slip 1 stitch, knit 1 stitch, pass the slipped stitch over the knit stitch, then knit to the end of the round.

10 Continue to decrease in this way on every other round until the total number of stitches remaining is equal to the number of stitches at the ankle (B).

11 Calculate the number of rounds you need to knit for the length of the foot and knit the foot without any further shaping, stopping at the beginning of the toe shaping. The length of the toe shaping should be the same measurement as the length of the heel flap.

12 The stitches are already divided up onto the three needles for the toe shaping with half of the stitches (the instep stitches) on needle 2 and the remaining stitches split equally across needles 1 and 3. Start decreasing at the beginning of the instep stitches on needle 2 as follows: knit 1 stitch, slip 1 stitch, knit 1 stitch, pass the slipped stitch over the knit stitch, knit until there are three stitches left on needle 2, knit two stitches together, knit 1 stitch. At the beginning of needle 3, knit 1 stitch, slip 1 stitch, knit 1 stitch, pass the slipped stitch over the knit stitch then work to the end of the stitches on the needle. Knit to the last 3 stitches on needle 1, knit two stitches together, knit one stitch.

13 Continue to decrease in this way on every other round for approximately four-fifths of the total length of the toe shaping, and then on every round until the width at the toe measures approximately 2.5 cm (1 in). Put the stitches on needles 1 and 3 onto one needle so that this needle and needle 2 have the same number of stitches on each of them. Hold the two sets of stitches side by side and knit them together.

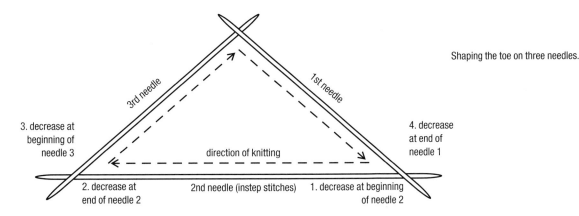

Shaping the toe on three needles.

Points to consider for socks

- Choose a yarn to knit socks that will not wear through too easily. Wool is a good yarn to use because it is strong and highly absorbent.

- It is a good idea to knit a welt at the top of the sock (A), so that the sock hugs the leg and doesn't fall down. Traditionally a rib is used because of its elasticity, however, any other firm stitch, such as moss/seed or garter stitch (see pages 16–18), could also be considered.

- Socks can be knitted in a variety of different stitches including ribs and Fair Isle. A ribbed fabric will stretch and recover well around the foot giving a comfortable fit, whereas a Fair Isle sock has less elasticity and will be less stretchy.

- Long socks need to be shaped between the top of the sock (A) and the ankle (B) to allow for the decrease in width along this length. Decreases should be made evenly, either side of a central stitch at the back of the calf (which will become the centre stitch on the heel flap), and should stop 2.5 cm (1 in) above the beginning of the heel flap.

- It is a good idea to use stitch markers to mark the beginning of a round (which will be the centre stitch at the back of the calf/heel flap), and where the decreases are going to be made for the instep and toe shaping.

- Slip the first stitch on every round of the heel flap so that it creates loops that can be used to pick up the stitches along both sides.

- When turning the heel, wrap a stitch before you turn to stop a hole from forming.

Slipover

A slipover is a garment without sleeves. It is usually quite close fitting, with or without side seam shaping and shaped shoulders. The armhole shaping on a slipover is deeper than the armhole shaping on a sweater with sleeves. This is because an allowance has to be made for the depth of the armhole bands. It is also important to remember that the shoulders should be knitted shorter, the back neck wider and the front neck deeper to allow for the depth of the bands.

How to design and knit a slipover

Back panel

1 Calculate the number of stitches you need to cast on for the width of the back panel (A).

2 Calculate the number of rows you need to knit for the length of the back panel (B), beginning after the welt.

3 Calculate the number of rows you need to knit for the length of the side seam (C), beginning after the welt.

4 The number of rows for the length of the side seam (C), subtracted from the number of rows for the length of the garment (B) will give you the number of rows for the armhole (D).

5 Calculate the number of stitches for the width of the back neck (J) and the shoulders (H).

6 The number of stitches in the back neck (J) added to the number of stitches in the two shoulders (H), subtracted from the number of stitches for the width of the back panel (A) will give you the number of stitches to decrease for both armholes.

7 Divide this number of stitches equally between the two armholes and begin by casting off half of these stitches at each side to create a small step (E).

8 Next create a smooth curve at each armhole (F) by decreasing one stitch at each end of every row for a few rows, and then one stitch at each end of every other row until the correct number of stitches have been decreased. Use proportional graph paper if necessary to help you work out a smooth curve.

9 Continue to knit straight to the beginning of the shoulder point (G).

10 Shape shoulders (H) by dividing the stitches for each of them into equal steps.

11 Cast/bind off the remaining stitches for the back neck (J).

Front panel

12 The front panel is knitted the same as the back panel, but the front neck shaping will need to be planned out. Advice on shaping necklines is given on pages 115–117.

How to join the panels

13 Join the shoulders.

14 Join the back and front side seams.

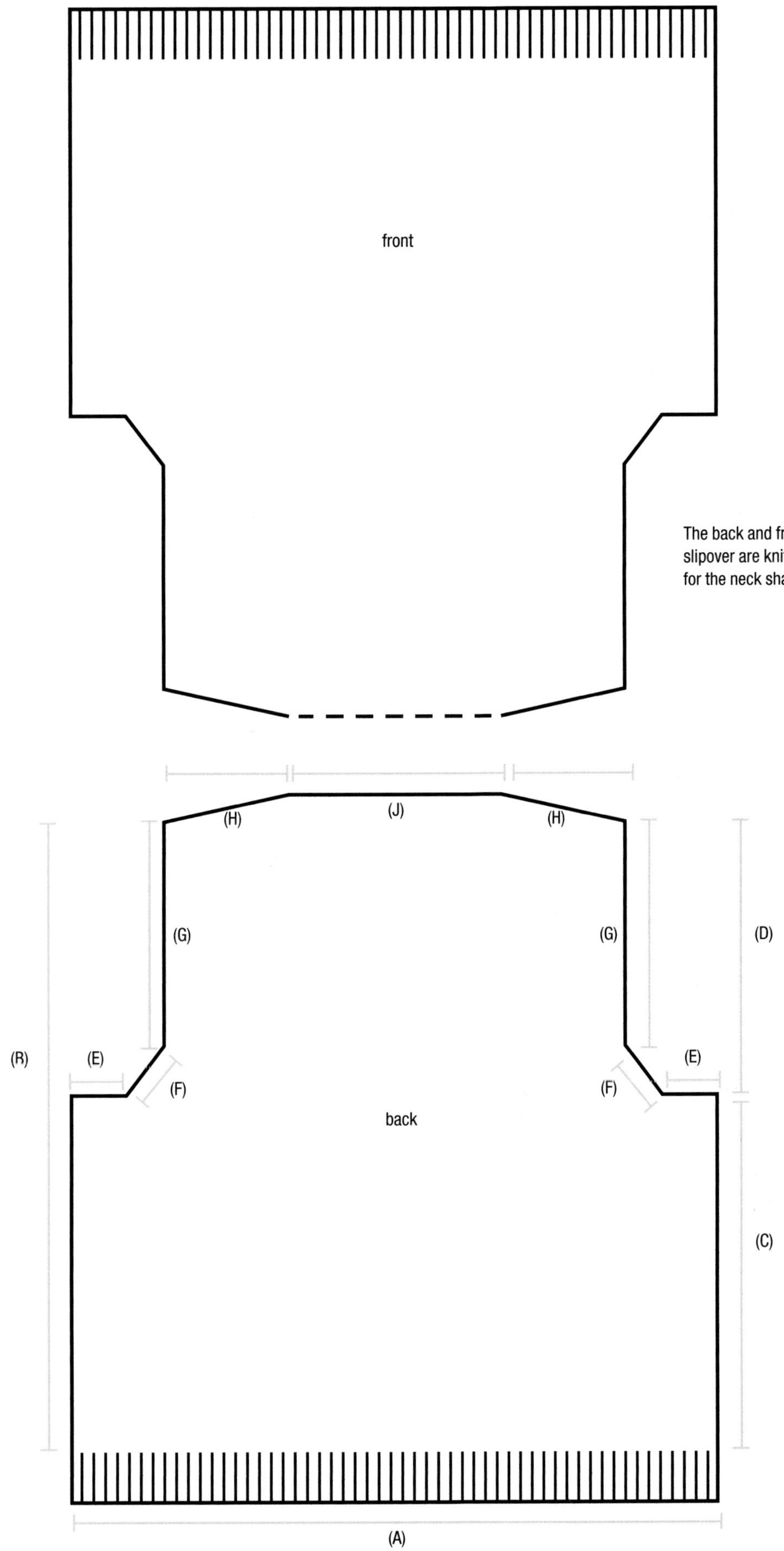

front

The back and front panels for a
slipover are knitted identically, except
for the neck shaping.

(H) (J) (H)

(G) (G) (D)

(R) (E) (E)

(F) (F)

back

(C)

(A)

Drop-shoulder sweater

A drop-shoulder sweater has very little shaping and is usually very generous in size, creating a loose-fitting garment that has a casual look. Because the shoulders drop down from the shoulder point, the sleeves are knitted to a shorter length than the sleeves for a set-in garment. Unlike other garments, it is not necessary to have a straight length knitted after the increases along the underarm of the sleeve because it will be sewn to a straight edge rather than into a shaped armhole. The shoulders can be straight or sloped.

How to design and knit a drop-shoulder sweater

Back panel

1 Calculate the number of stitches you need to cast on for the width of the back panel (A).

2 Calculate the number of rows you need to knit for the length of the back panel (B), beginning after the welt.

3 Calculate the number of stitches for the width of the shoulders (C) and the back neck (D).

4 Mark the back neck width (D) and cast/bind off the stitches for both shoulders and the back neck.

Front panel

5 The front panel is knitted the same as the back panel, but the front neck shaping will need to be planned out. Advice on shaping necklines is given on pages 115–117.

Sleeves

6 Calculate the number of stitches you need to cast on for the width of the sleeve at the cuff (E).

7 Calculate the number of stitches you need for the width at the top of the sleeve (G).

8 Calculate the number of rows you need to knit for the length of the sleeve (F), beginning after the welt.

9 Work out the number of paired increases (see pages 70–71) needed to shape the sleeve. Alternatively, proportional graph paper can be used to help you work out a smooth diagonal slant.

10 After all of the shaping has been completed and the sleeve is the correct length, cast/bind off stitches (G).

How to join the panels

11 Join the shoulders.

12 Mark the centre point of each sleeve along the cast/bind-off edge at the top (G).

13 Sew the sleeves to the back and front panels, matching the marked centre point on the sleeves to the shoulder seams so that they are sewn in equally.

14 Join the back and front side seams and the underarm seams from hem to wrist.

Yarn choice

This type of garment results in a "sloppy joe" style which is completely unfitted and usually over generous in size. Because of this you need to think carefully about the weight of yarn that you choose to knit up a drop-shoulder sweater because the overall weight of the finished garment could end up being very heavy. Also, due to the omission of shaping at the top of the sleeve and the armhole, extra folds of fabric will be created here when the garment is worn, and this will be more emphasised if a chunky yarn is used to knit it up.

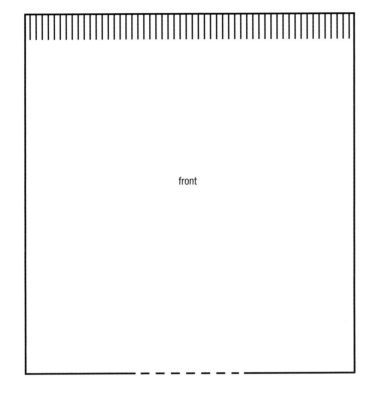

front

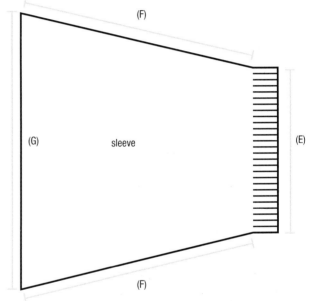

(F)

(G) sleeve (E)

(F)

There is very little shaping on a drop shoulder sweater and this gives it a casual look.

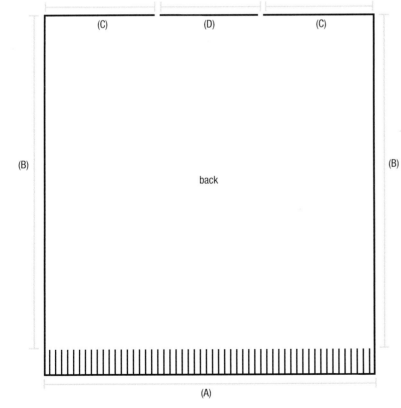

(C) (D) (C)

(B) (B)

back

(A)

Sweater with a simple set-in sleeve

This sweater has a little bit more shaping than the drop-shoulder sweater, creating a slightly more fitted garment. However, despite the sloped shoulders and the shaping at the beginning of the armhole, the shoulders will still drop down from the shoulder point. The extra folds of fabric at the underarm created by the drop of the shoulder and the wide panels will be slightly reduced by the straight section at the top of the sleeve, allowing better ease of movement.

   The sleeves should have the same number of centimetres/inches added to their length as the inset at the beginning of the armhole shaping to ensure that they are the correct length.

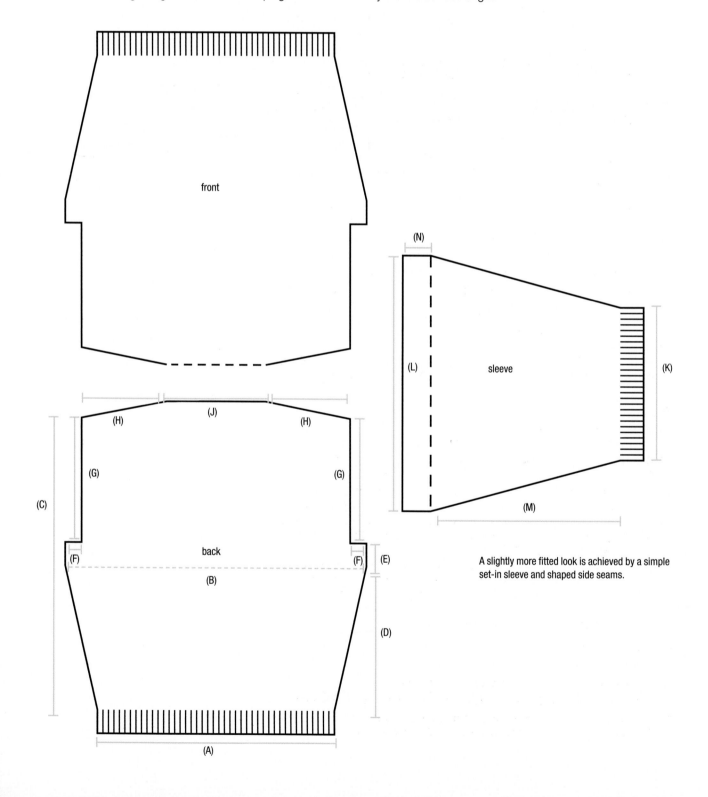

A slightly more fitted look is achieved by a simple set-in sleeve and shaped side seams.

How to design and knit a sweater with a simple set-in sleeve

Back panel

1 Calculate the number of stitches you need to cast on for the width of the back panel (A).

2 Calculate the number of stitches you need for the width of the back panel (B).

3 Calculate the number of rows you need to knit for the length of the back panel (C), beginning after the welt.

4 Calculate the number of rows you need to knit for the length of the side seam (D), beginning after the welt and finishing at the dotted line as indicated on the spec.

5 Calculate the number of rows you need to knit for the length of the short straight section between the dotted line and the beginning of the armhole shaping (E). (E should measure a minimum of 2.5 cm (1 in).)

6 The number of rows for the side seam (D), added to the number of rows for the straight section (E), subtracted from the number of rows for the length of the back panel (C) will give you the number of rows for the armhole (G).

7 Work out the number of paired increases (see pages 70–71) needed to shape the side edges between the top of the welt and the dotted line (D). Alternatively, proportional graph paper can be used to help you work out a smooth diagonal slant.

8 Calculate the number of stitches for the back neck (J) and the shoulders (H).

9 The number of stitches in the back neck (J) added to the number of stitches in the two shoulders (H), subtracted from the number of stitches for the width of the back panel (A) will give you the number of stitches to cast/bind off at the beginning of both armholes. (This should measure approximately 2 cm (¾ in) at each side.)

10 Divide this number of stitches equally between the two armholes and cast them off to create a small step (F).

11 Continue to knit straight to the beginning of the shoulder point (G).

12 Shape shoulders (H) by dividing the stitches for each of them into equal steps.

13 Cast/bind off the remaining stitches for the back neck (J) or leave them on a holder.

Front panel

14 The front panel is knitted the same as the back panel, but the front neck shaping will need to be planned out. Advice on shaping necklines is given on pages 115–117.

Sleeves

15 Calculate the number of stitches you need to cast on for the width of the sleeve at the cuff (K).

16 Calculate the number of stitches you need for the width at the top of the sleeve (L).

17 Calculate the number of rows you need to knit for the length of the sleeve (M), beginning after the welt and finishing at the dotted line as indicated on the spec.

18 Calculate the number of rows you need to knit for the length of the short straight section between the dotted line and the beginning of the sleeve shaping (N). (N should measure a minimum of 2.5 cm (1 in).)

19 Work out the number of paired increases (see pages 70–71) needed to shape the sleeve between the top of the cuff and the dotted line (M). Alternatively, proportional graph paper can be used to help you work out a smooth diagonal slant.

20 Cast/bind off stitches (L).

How to join the panels

21 Join the shoulders.

22 Join the back and front side seams and the underarm seams.

23 Mark the centre point of each sleeve along the cast/bind-off edge at the top (L).

24 Set in the sleeves by sewing the cast/bind-off edge into the armholes, matching the marked centre point on the sleeves to the shoulder seams.

Sweater with a set-in sleeve

A sweater with a set-in sleeve is usually either fitted or semi-fitted, with the armholes, the tops of the sleeves, the shoulders and sometimes the side seams too, being shaped.

The curved shape at the top of the sleeve is referred to as the 'cap' and the higher the cap is, the more fitted the sleeve will be. The height of the cap is designed to match the circumference of the armhole so that the two panels fit together perfectly. Therefore the width at the top of the sleeve, the depth of the armhole and the shape of the cap are all crucial measurements for this style of garment and they must be measured carefully to ensure a precise fit.

The shaping might seem tricky to work out at first, but with proportional graph paper, these simple guidelines and a bit of string (see String thing, page 100), the shape of the armhole and the cap can be worked out quite easily.

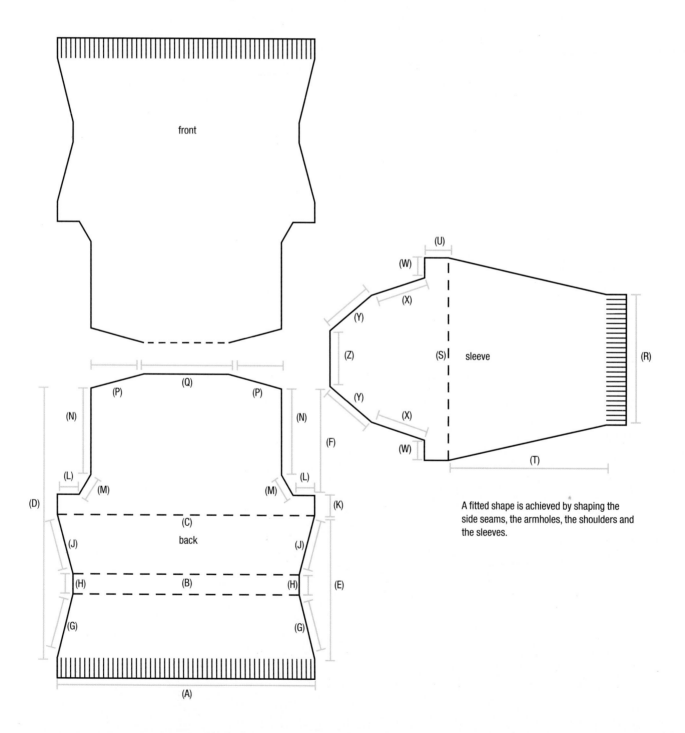

A fitted shape is achieved by shaping the side seams, the armholes, the shoulders and the sleeves.

How to design and knit a sweater with a set-in sleeve

Back panel

1 Calculate the number of stitches you need to cast on for the width of the back panel (A), the number of stitches to decrease down to at the waist (B), and the number of stitches to increase out to at the bust point (C).

2 Calculate the number of rows you need to knit for the length of the back panel (D), beginning after the welt.

3 Calculate the number of rows you need for the length of the side seam (E), beginning after the welt and finishing at the dotted line as indicated on the spec.

4 Calculate the number of rows you need to knit for the length of the short straight section between the dotted line and the beginning of the armhole shaping (K). (K should measure a minimum of 2.5 cm (1 in).)

5 The number of rows for the side seam (E), added to the number of rows for the straight section (K), subtracted from the number of rows for the length of the back panel (D) will give you the number of rows for the armhole (F).

6 Work out the number of paired decreases (see pages 70–71) needed to shape the side edges to the waist (G), stopping at the first dotted line. The straight section (H) should measure a minimum of 2.5 cm (1 in). Then calculate the number of paired increases needed to shape the side edges from the second dotted line up to the third dotted line (J).

7 Calculate the number of stitches for the back neck (Q) and the shoulders (P).

8 The number of stitches in the back neck (Q) added to the number of stitches in the two shoulders (P), subtracted from the number of stitches at the bust/chest point (C) will give you the number of stitches to cast/bind off for both armholes. (This should be approximately 2 cm (¾ in).)

9 Divide this number of stitches equally between the two armholes and begin by casting/binding off a few of them at each side to create a small step (L).

10 Next create a smooth curve at each armhole by decreasing one stitch at each end of every row for a few rows, and then one stitch at each end of every other row until the correct number of stitches has been decreased (M). How often you decrease will depend on the number of rows available and the number of stitches that need to be discarded. Use proportional graph paper if necessary to help you work out a smooth curve.

11 Continue to knit straight to the beginning of the shoulder shaping (N).

12 Shape shoulders (P) by dividing the stitches for them into equal steps.

13 Cast/bind off the remaining stitches for the back neck (Q).

Front panel

14 The front panel is knitted the same as the back panel, but the front neck shaping will need to be planned out. Advice on shaping necklines is given on pages 115–117.

Sleeves

15 Calculate the number of stitches you need to cast on for the width of the sleeve at the cuff (R).

16 Calculate the number of stitches you need for the width at the top of the sleeve (S).

17 Calculate the number of rows you need to knit for the length of the sleeve (T), beginning after the welt and finishing at the dotted line as indicated on the spec.

18 Calculate the number of rows you need to knit for the length of the short straight section between the dotted line and the beginning of the sleeve shaping (U). (U should measure a minimum of 2.5 cm (1 in).)

19 Work out the number of paired increases (see pages 70–71) needed to shape the sleeve between the top of the cuff and the dotted line (T). Alternatively, proportional graph paper can be used to help you work out a smooth diagonal slant.

20 Cast/bind off the same number of stitches at the beginning of the sleeve cap as you cast/bind off at the beginning of the armhole shaping to create a small step at each side (W to match L).

21 Decrease stitches on every row to shape the lower half of the sleeve cap (X).

How to design and knit a sweater with a set-in sleeve, cont...

22 Continue to decrease at each edge on every other row for several rows, then on every row again (Y) until the width of the cap (Z) is approximately 7.5 cm (3 in) (adult) or 5 cm (2 in) (child). If the shape of the curve is looking too angular, try mapping it out onto proportional graph paper and revising the decreases. As a general guide, the height of the cap is usually about two-thirds of the length of the armhole.

23 When you are knitting the cap you can check whether the cap will fit into the armhole by measuring the length of the cap and comparing it to the circumference of the armhole (front and back). If the cap is the same length or slightly longer than the armhole, cast/bind off the remaining stitches (Z). If the measurement of the cap is shorter than the armhole, work a few more rows before casting off.

How to join the panels

24 Join the shoulders.

25 Join the back and front side seams and the underarm seams.

26 Mark the centre point of each sleeve along the cast/bind-off edge of the cap (Z). Set in the sleeves by sewing them into the armhole, matching the marked centre point on the cap to the shoulder seams.

27 Ease any extra fabric around the cap into the top of the shoulder.

String thing

There is another quick and easy way to work out how to shape the sleeve cap. First, measure the circumference of the actual armhole with a piece of string. Cut the string to this length plus 1 cm (½ in) and mark the middle of it. Next, draw a horizontal line onto a piece of paper that is equal in measurement to the width at the top of the sleeve (before the shaping of the cap begins). Draw a vertical line through the horizontal line, crossing it at the centre point. Lay the string onto the paper, so that each end of it touches the start and finish of the horizontal line. Adjust the string until it makes a smooth curve on the paper, making sure that the middle of the string hits the vertical line. When you are happy with the shape of the curve draw around the string and then transfer the curve onto proportional graph paper, making sure that the shape of it is the same on both sides of the vertical line. Finally, square off the stitches so that you can see where the decreases need to be made (see page 36), and cast/bind off the remaining stitches along the top edge. This way you can be sure that the measurement of the cap matches the circumference of the armhole.

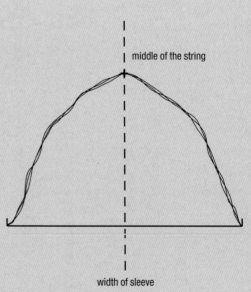

middle of the string

width of sleeve

How to work out the shape of the sleeve cap with string.

Sweater with a set-in raglan

A raglan sweater has diagonal lines of decreases on the sleeves and the front and back panels and they fit together perfectly to create a garment that can be either loose-fitting or close-fitting. This type of garment does not have an 'armhole' as such, and there are no shoulder seams.

The raglan shaping on the body panels continues right up to the neck edge, while the raglan shaping on the sleeves is worked to match the back and front panels and then the remaining stitches left over at the top of the sleeves are cast/bind off. These cast/bind-off edges form part of the neckline on both the front and the back of the garment.

The decreases on the sleeves and body panels should be identical if possible, and if they are uniform (in other words, they are equally spaced with the same number of rows between decreases), then a rounded shoulder shape will be created.

If the decreases are varied with a steeper slope at the top of the sleeve, then the shape will be more angular around the shoulder.

The following example shows a raglan with uniform decreasing and a choice of two possible methods for working out the raglan shaping.

How to design and knit a sweater with a set-in raglan: method 1

Back panel

1 Calculate the number of stitches you need to cast on for the width of the back panel (A).

2 Calculate the number of rows you need to knit for the length of the back panel (B), beginning after the welt.

3 Calculate the number of rows you need to knit for the length of the side seam (C), beginning after the welt.

4 The number of rows for the side seam (C), subtracted from the number of rows for the length of the back panel (B) will give you the number of rows for the armhole (D).

5 Plot out the raglan shaping onto proportional graph paper by first mapping out the width of the back panel (A), the depth of the armhole (D), and the width of the back neck (G). (The back neck width should be a minimum of 13 cm (5 in) for a close-fitting neckline, bearing in mind that half of the cast/bind-off edge at the top of the sleeve (Q) will create part of the back neck width.) The width of the back neck (G) subtracted from the width of the back panel (A) will give you the number of stitches to decrease for both raglans. Divide this number of stitches equally in half.

6 Cast/bind off a few stitches at the beginning of the raglan shaping at each side (approximately 2 cm (¾ in)) to create a small step (E), then draw a diagonal line on the proportional graph paper, joining the end of the cast/bind off steps (E) to the back neck (G), this is shown on the spec as a dotted line. Draw in the decreases. (Alternatively, the paired decreases for the raglan can be calculated using the formula on pages 70–71.)

7 If the decreases are not working out satisfactorily you might have to alter the length of the raglan (F) by changing the width of the body (A) and/or the width of the back neck (G).

8 When the raglan shaping is completed cast/bind off the stitches for the back neck (G).

Front panel

9 The front panel is knitted the same as the back panel, but the front neck shaping will need to be planned out. Advice on shaping necklines is given on pages 115–117.

10 The length of the raglan on the front panel (R) might work out to be shorter than the raglan on the back panel (F), depending on the diagonal slope of it and where it cuts into the neckline (this will be determined when the front neck shaping is drawn onto the proportional graph paper).

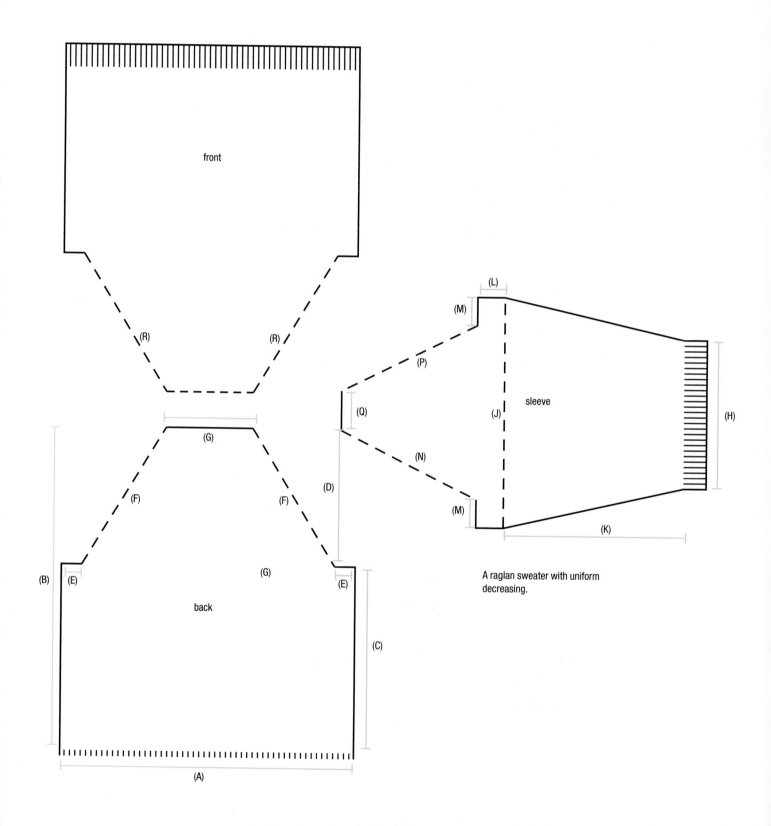

A raglan sweater with uniform decreasing.

Sleeves

11 Calculate the number of stitches you need to cast on for the width of the sleeve at the cuff (H).

12 Calculate the number of stitches you need for the width at the top of the sleeve (J).

13 Calculate the number of rows you need to knit for the length of the sleeve (K), beginning after the welt and finishing at the dotted line as indicated on the spec.

14 Calculate the number of rows you need to knit for the length of the short straight section between the dotted line and the beginning of the sleeve shaping (L). (L should measure a minimum of 2.5 cm (1 in).)

15 Work out the number of paired increases (see pages 70–71) needed to shape the sleeve between the top of the cuff and the dotted line (K). Alternatively proportional graph paper can be used to help you work out a smooth diagonal slant.

16 Plot out the raglan shaping on proportional graph paper by first mapping out the width at the top of the sleeve (J) and then draw in the diagonal line on both sides (N and P) (this is shown on the spec as a dotted line). Make sure that the diagonal lines are the same length as the back and front panels, copying the decreases and the cast/bind-off steps at the beginning of the raglan shaping like for like. It is crucial that the shaping of the raglans on both sides of the sleeve matches the shaping of the raglans on the back and front panels so that they fit together perfectly (N to match F and P to match R).

17 When all of the decreases have been drawn in and the raglan is the same number of rows on each side as the front and back panels, cast/bind off the remaining stitches at the top (Q). The number of stitches at this point will vary depending on the width of the sleeve, but the measurement should be no less than 2.5 cm (1 in). If the measurement is greater than this, then the top edge of the sleeve (Q) should be shaped with a slight rise towards the back. This will lengthen the raglan on the back panel and the sleeve (F and N) and consequently it will shorten the width of the back neck, which will then have to be re-drawn onto the proportional graph paper. A left sleeve and a right sleeve will be created, rather than two identical sleeves.

18 Calculate the measurement of the circumference of the neckline to ensure that it is wide enough to fit over the head. If it is coming up a bit short, keep the raglan shaping on all of the panels the same but increase the width of the sleeves and the front and back panels, and this in turn will increase the circumference of the neckline. The pattern will then have to be re-drawn onto proportional graph paper.

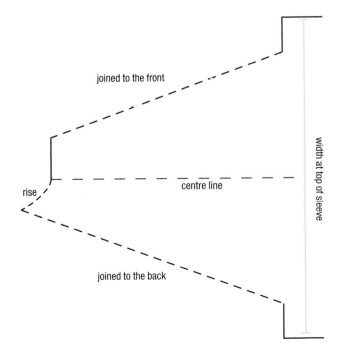

joined to the front

rise

centre line

joined to the back

width at top of sleeve

Top of a raglan sleeve with a rise towards the back.

How to design and knit a sweater with a set-in raglan: method 2

To calculate the raglan shaping for the front and back panels, this method starts by working out the calculations for the neckline and working down towards the beginning of the raglan shaping on both front and back panels and the sleeves. This method ensures that the neckline is the correct measurement. However, the sweater is still knitted in the conventional way from bottom to top.

The neckline divided up into sections for raglan shaping.

Back panel

1–4 Follow instructions **1–4** for method 1.

5 Decide on the shape and circumference of the whole neckline. Sketch the neckline onto plain paper and plan how many centimetres/inches are in each section.

6 Make sure that the total measurement around the neckline is enough for the head to be able to pass through. For a close-fitting neckline the back neck should be no less than 13 cm (5 in) and the width at the top of each sleeve where they meet the neckline should be no less than 2.5 cm (1 in) – this will make a total of 15.5 cm (6 in) for the back neck width. The width of the back neck (G) added to the width at the top of both sleeves where they meet the neckline (Q), subtracted from the circumference of the neckline will give you the width of the front neck opening.

7 Calculate the number of stitches for the whole neckline and draw it out onto proportional graph paper.

8 Measure the depth of the armhole straight (D), not along the diagonal slope of the raglan.

9 Plot out the raglan shaping onto proportional graph paper by first mapping out the depth of the armhole (D) and the width of the back panel (A). Then, beginning at the neck edge, draw a diagonal line joining these points, remembering that a few stitches at the beginning of the raglan shaping at each side of the armhole will be cast/bind off straight (E) to create a small step (approximately 2 cm (¾ in)).

10 Draw in the increases. (Alternatively, the increases for the diagonal slope can be calculated using the formula on page 70–71.)

11 If the decreases are not working out satisfactorily you might have to alter the length of the raglan (F) by changing the width of the body (A).

Sleeves

12–16 Follow instructions **11–15** for method 1.

17 Plot out the raglan shaping onto proportional graph paper by drawing in the diagonal lines on both sides (N and P), beginning at the neck edge and working down towards the armhole. Make sure that the diagonal lines are the same length as the back and front panels, copying the decreases and the cast/bind-off steps at the beginning of the raglan shaping like for like. Remember that the length of the raglan on the front panel (R) might end up being shorter than the length of the raglan on the back panel (F), and if this is the case, the same shaping must be imitated on the sleeves to match the back and front panels (N to match F and P to match R). This will create a left sleeve and a right sleeve rather than two identical sleeves.

18 The width of the sleeve (J) might have to be altered to keep the raglan shaping on the sleeves and body panels identical.

How to join the panels: both methods

19 Sew the raglans together by joining each sleeve to the front and back panels.

20 Sew the back and front side seams and the underarm seams together from hem to wrist.

Sweater with a saddle shoulder

A sweater with a saddle shoulder is designed in the same way as a sweater with a set-in sleeve, but a shoulder yoke is created at the top of the sleeve cap. The length of the armholes is shortened to accommodate the width of the shoulder yoke so that it fits perfectly into the front and back panels. This creates a flat, square shape at the top of the garment that gives it a 'military' look. It is generally used for men's sweaters rather than those for women.

How to design and knit a sweater with saddle shoulder

Back panel

1 Calculate the number of stitches you need to cast on for the width of the back panel (A).

2 Calculate the number of rows you need to knit for the depth of (J). (The depth of (J) measures the same as the width at the top of the shoulder yoke (U), divided by two.)

3 Calculate the number of rows you need to knit for the length of the back panel (B), beginning after the welt.

4 Calculate the number of rows you need to knit for the length of the side seam (C), beginning after the welt.

5 The number of rows for the length of the back panel (B), minus the number of rows for the length of the side seam (C), will give you the number of rows for the armhole (D).

6 Calculate the number of stitches for the width of the back neck (K) and the width of the cast/bind-off edges where they meet the shoulder yokes (H).

7 The number of stitches in the back neck (K) added to the cast/bind-off stitches (H), subtracted from the number of stitches for the width (A) will give you the number of stitches to decrease at both armholes.

8 Divide this number of stitches equally between the two armholes and cast/bind off a few of them (approximately 2 cm (¾ in)) at the beginning of the next two rows to create a small step at each side (E).

9 Next, create a smooth curve at each armhole by decreasing one stitch at each end of every row for a few rows, and then one stitch at each end of every other row until the correct number of stitches have been decreased (F). How often you decrease will depend on the number of rows available and the number of stitches that need to be discarded. Use proportional graph paper if necessary to help you work out a smooth curve.

10 Continue to knit straight to the beginning of the cast/bind-off stitches for the shoulder yokes (G).

11 Cast/bind off the stitches for the shoulder yokes (H).

12 Continue to knit straight to the beginning of the back neck (J).

13 Cast/bind off the remaining stitches for the back neck (K).

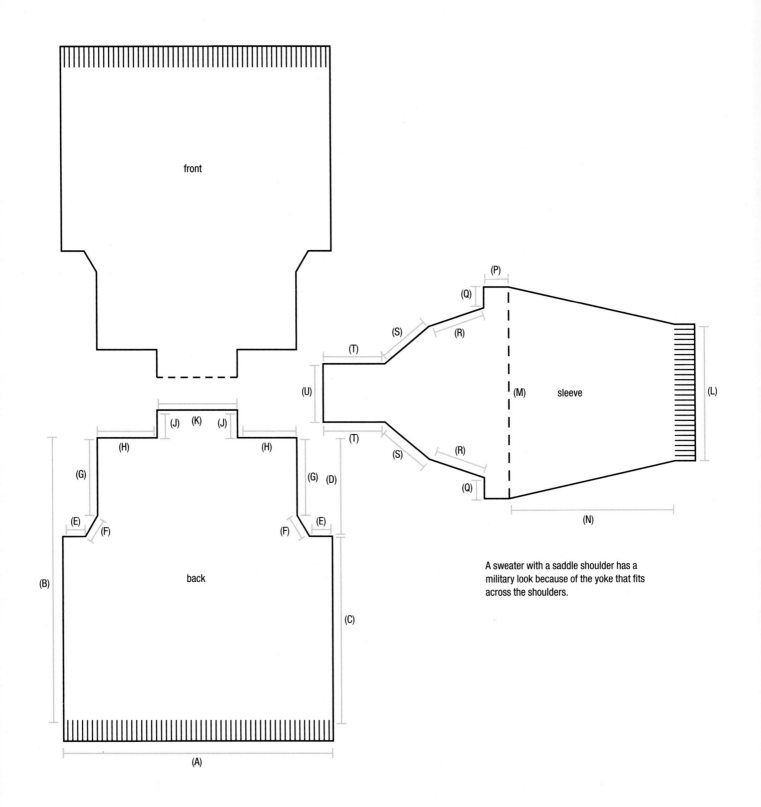

front

(P)

(Q)

(S)

(R)

(T)

(U)

(M) sleeve

(L)

(T)

(S)

(R)

(Q)

(N)

A sweater with a saddle shoulder has a military look because of the yoke that fits across the shoulders.

(J) (K) (J)

(H) (H)

(G) (G) (D)

(E) (E)

(F) (F)

(B) back

(C)

(A)

Front panel

14 The front panel is knitted the same as the back panel, but the front neck shaping will need to be planned out. Advice on shaping necklines is given on pages 117.

Sleeves

15 Calculate the number of stitches you need to cast on for the width of the sleeve at the cuff (L).

16 Calculate the number of stitches you need for the width at the top of the sleeve (M).

17 Calculate the number of rows you need to knit for the length of the sleeve (N), beginning after the welt and finishing at the dotted line as indicated on the spec.

18 Calculate the number of rows you need to knit for the length of the short straight section between the dotted line and the beginning of the sleeve shaping (P). (P should measure a minimum of 2.5 cm (1 in)).

19 Work out the number of paired increases (see pages 70–71) needed to shape the sleeve between the top of the cuff and the dotted line. Alternatively proportional graph paper can be used to help you work out a smooth diagonal slant.

20 Cast/bind off the same number of stitches at the beginning of the sleeve cap as you cast/bind off at the beginning of the armhole shaping to create a small step at each side (Q to match E).

21 Decrease stitches on every row to shape the lower half of the sleeve cap (R).

22 Continue to decrease at each edge on every other row for several rows, then on every row again (S) until the width at the top of the cap is the desired width for the shoulder yoke (U). If the shape of the curve is looking too angular, try mapping it out onto proportional graph paper and revising the decreases.

23 When you are knitting the cap you can check whether it will fit into the armhole by measuring the length of the cap (excluding the stitches for the shoulder yoke) and comparing it to the circumference of the armhole (front and back, excluding the width of the shoulder yoke). If the cap is the same length or slightly longer than the armhole, then you can begin to knit the shoulder yoke. If the measurement of the cap is shorter than the armhole, work a few more rows before shaping the shoulder yoke.

24 Calculate the number of rows you need to knit for the shoulder yoke (T), so that it fits perfectly into the front and back panels (T to match H).

25 Cast/bind off stitches (U). If the width of the shoulder yoke measures no more than 2.5 cm (1 in), then the stitches can be cast/bind off straight. However, if the width of the shoulder yoke is greater than this, it should be shaped with a slight rise towards the back. This will lengthen the shoulder yoke at the back (T), which means that the width of the cast/bind-off steps on the back panel (H) will also have to be altered. Consequently the width of the back neck will be shortened and will have to be re-drawn. A left sleeve and a right sleeve will be created, rather than two identical sleeves.

How to join the panels

26 Join the back and front side seams and the underarm seams.

27 Set in the sleeves and shoulder yokes to the front and back panels.

Sweater with a circular yoke

The back, front and sleeve panels of this type of sweater can be knitted on straight needles up to the point where the yoke begins. Then it is best to put all of the stitches onto a circular needle (or double-pointed needles) and knit the yoke in one panel in the round.

The yoke is shaped to accommodate the shoulders and the upper half of the body, so this means that there are no shoulder seams. The stitches for the yoke need to be decreased at regular intervals between the beginning of the yoke and the neck edge. These decreases need to be carefully calculated so that they are distributed evenly around the yoke, finishing at the neck edge with the correct number of stitches for the circumference of the neckline.

Because the yoke is worked in the round, the shape of the neckline on this type of sweater is usually round as well. The yoke can be as deep as you want it to be, and it will work with most types of sleeve.

This example is worked as if a set-in sleeve-style were being knitted, but the yoke begins after the shaping at the beginning of the armhole on both the back and front panels and the same amount of shaping of the sleeve cap on each sleeve have all been completed.

How to design and knit a sweater with a circular yoke

Back panel (up to the yoke)

1 Draw a spec of the back panel of a sweater with a set-in raglan sleeve (see page 98). Omit the waist shaping of the body panels so that they are straight (C), (unless you want the garment to be fitted).

2 Calculate the number of rows you need to knit for the depth of the yoke, measuring it from the back neck. The deeper the yoke is, the more it will cut across the sleeve panels, thus creating a wider looking 'shoulder'.

3 Mark the depth of the yoke onto the spec so that you can work out where it cuts across the armhole. On this example the yoke begins after the decreases have been completed at the beginning of the armhole shaping (after E). Use proportional graph paper if necessary to help you plan this out.

4 Knit the back panel up to where the yoke begins (after the armhole shaping on this example, as indicated by a dotted line on the spec), and leave the stitches on a holder.

5 The remaining shaping of the upper half of the back panel (F, G and H) is eliminated. It is shown on the spec as a shaded area.

Front panel (up to the yoke)

6 The front panel needs to be planned out and knitted the same as the back panel, leaving the stitches on a holder after the armhole shaping has been completed. The amount of stitches for the circumference of the neckline will be calculated later on.

Sleeves (up to the yoke)

7 Draw a spec of a set-in raglan sleeve (see page 98).

8 Mark a line on the spec to indicate where the yoke will cut across the sleeve cap, making sure that it matches the yoke on the back and front panels. In this example the yoke begins after the shaping has begun at the beginning of the cap and is indicated by a dotted line on the spec.

9 Knit the sleeve up to where the yoke begins (after the shaping at the beginning of the cap as indicated on the spec), and leave the stitches on holders.

10 Work both sleeves the same, leaving the stitches on holders.

11 The remaining shaping of the upper half of the sleeve cap (part of P, Q and R) is eliminated. It is shown on the spec as a shaded area.

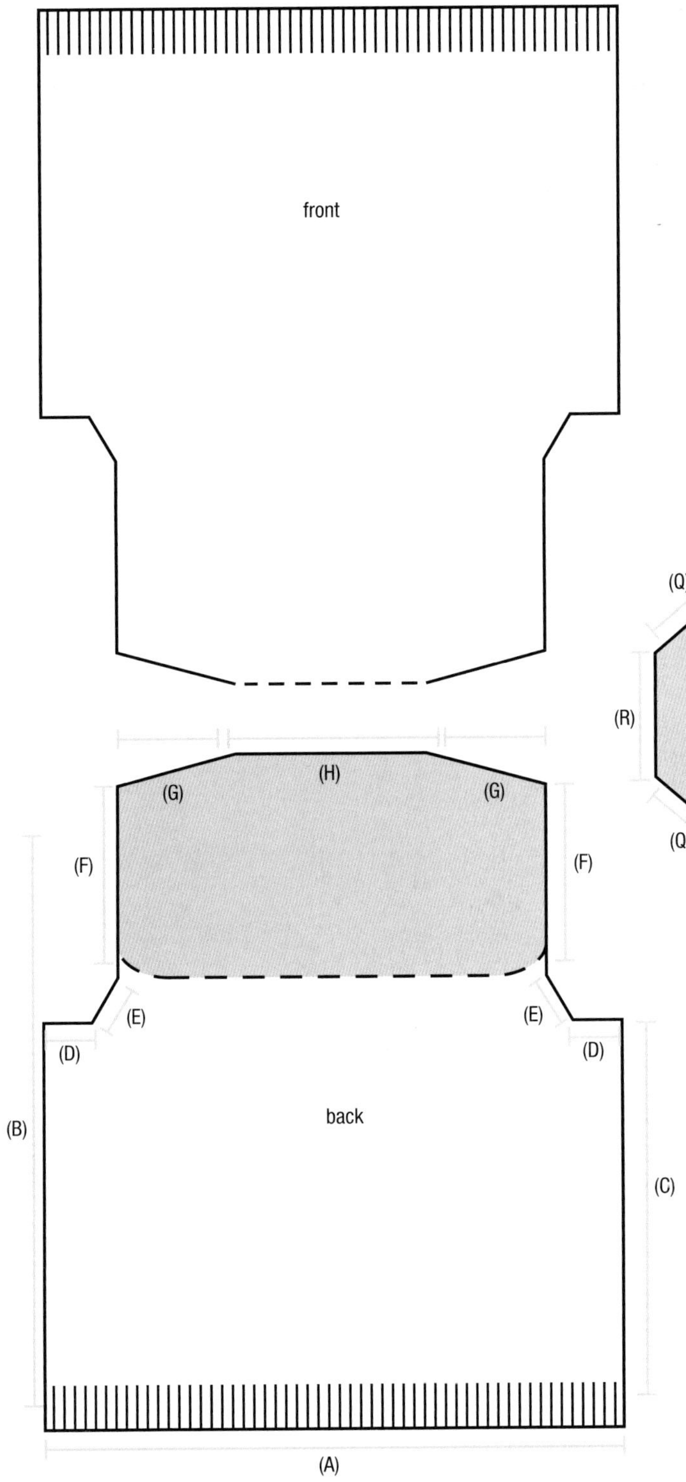

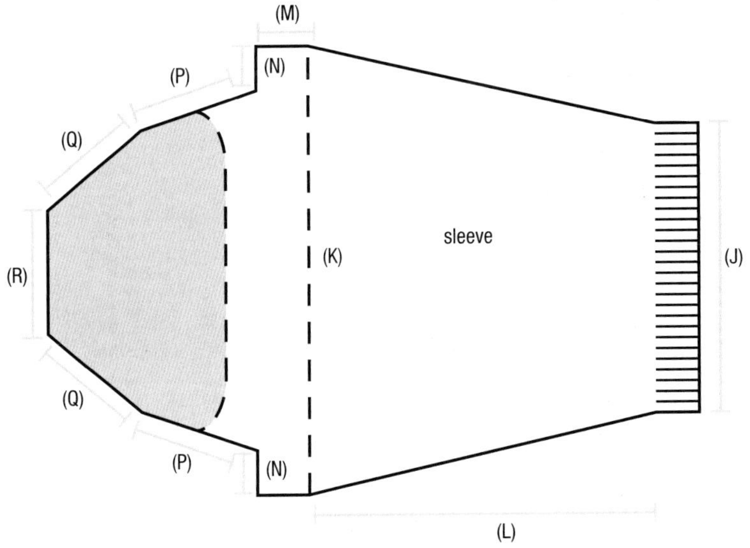

front

(M)

(P) (N)

(Q)

(R) sleeve (K) (J)

(Q)

(P) (N)

(L)

(H)

(G) (G)

(F) (F)

(E) (E)

(D) (D)

(B) back

(C)

(A)

A sweater with a circular yoke can be started on straight needles but the stitches will have to be swapped onto circular or double-pointed needles to complete the yokes.

The yoke

12 Decide on the measurement of the circumference of the neckline, making sure that it is wide enough for the head to pass through it.

13 Calculate the number of stitches you need for the circumference of the neckline.

14 Count the number of stitches that are on holders for the back and front panels and both sleeves.

15 Subtract the number of stitches calculated for the neckline from the total number of stitches on holders. This gives you the amount of stitches that need to be decreased around the yoke.

16 Work out an even distribution of the decreases across the number of rows calculated for the depth of the yoke, leaving at least one row between each decrease row. At the same time you need to decide how many decreases are going to be made across a row and where the decreases are going to be worked. The plotting of the decreases for the yoke might be easier to work out on proportional graph paper or on a diagram (see diagram below).

17 Place the panels in the correct order on a circular needle, (back panel, one sleeve, front panel, then the other sleeve panel), and continue the work in the round, placing markers on the first round to indicate where the decreases are going to be made so that they can be worked at the same point on every decrease row.

18 In this example a total of 12 stitches would be decreased on every decrease row. The number of rounds between the decrease rows is determined by the total number of rows calculated for the depth of the yoke. If the mathematics are not working out precisely, then you will have to alter either the depth of the yoke, or the width of the back, front and/or sleeve panels to make the calculations work.

How to join the panels

19 Join the back and front side seams and the underarm seams. Alternatively, these seams can be joined before the yoke is knitted.

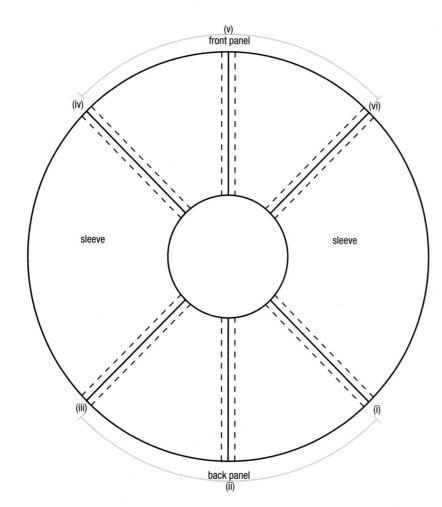

The diagram shows the yoke broken down into sections to suggest where the decreases could be worked. This example has double decreases (indicated by dashes), either side of the following marked points:

Where the sleeve meets the back panel (i).

At the centre back (ii).

Where the back panel meets the sleeve (iii).

Where the sleeve meets the front panel (iv).

At the centre front (v).

Where the front panel meets the sleeve (vi).

Jacket/cardigan

Almost any sweater design can be converted into a jacket or cardigan
quite easily.

1 On all styles the front panel is divided in half along the centre to make an opening,
but the sleeve panels and the back panel remain unchanged.

2 The two panels created by dividing the front panel in half are referred to as the
'left front' and the 'right front'. The number of stitches for each of these panels
should be the same, so there must be an even number of stitches in the front
panel before it is divided in half.

3 Both edges of the left and right front panels are usually finished with a band in a
firm stitch, such as rib, garter or moss/seed (see pages 38–39), to stabilize them
and stop them from curling back on themselves. This can be knitted integrally,
knitted separately and sewn on, or picked up.

4 If the width of the front bands is minimal (less than 1.25 cm (½ in)), the front
panel can be divided in half and no allowance needs to be made for the width of
them. However, if the bands are wider than this, the width of each front panel
should be decreased to make an allowance for them. But remember that
because the bands cross over each other at the front (unless it is an edge-to-
edge garment) each front panel only needs to be reduced by half the combined
width of the bands.

5 To plan out the design of a jacket/cardigan, choose the shape that you want and
first of all draw the spec as a sweater, including the neckline. Then map out onto
the spec of the front panel the divide up the centre to create the left and right
front panels. If necessary, re-draw the lines for both centre front edges, making
an allowance for the front bands.

6 In this example the width of the front bands is going to be 2.5 cm (1 in), so the left
and right front panels have to be decreased in width by 1.25 cm (½ in) (shown on
the diagram as two solid lines either side of the dotted line).

7 This also means that the total circumference of the front neck has been reduced
by 2.5 cm (1 in), or 1.25 cm (½ in) when the garment is buttoned up.

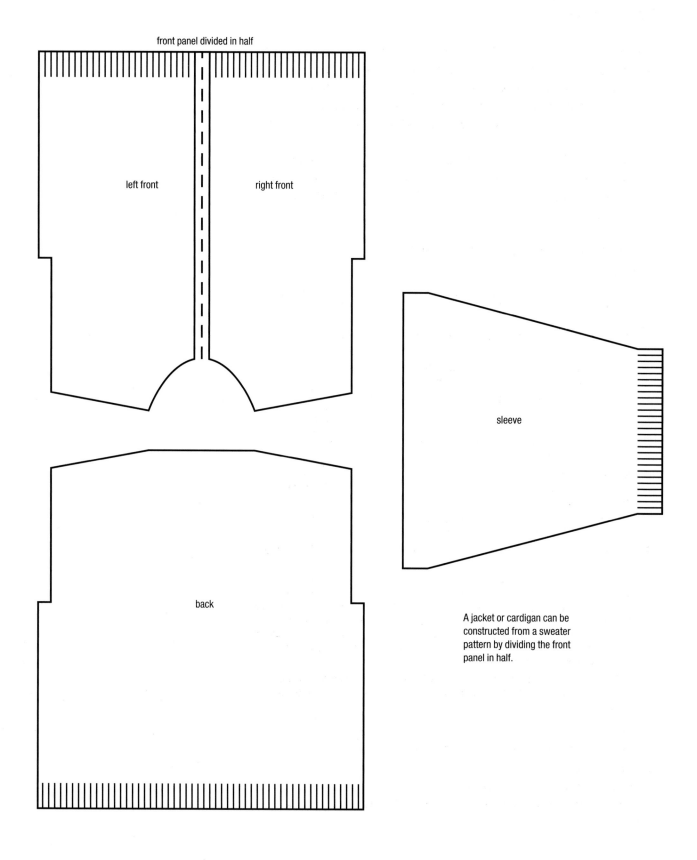

front panel divided in half

left front

right front

sleeve

back

A jacket or cardigan can be constructed from a sweater pattern by dividing the front panel in half.

Straight skirt

The quality of the fabric for a knitted skirt should be firm rather than loose (see page 57), and a durable yarn is recommended, rather than a soft, fragile yarn, to help prevent the knitting being stretched too much through general wear.

To help stabilize the bottom edge of the skirt and taper it in slightly, the first few centimetres/inches could be knitted on a smaller needle and in a firm stitch, such as rib, garter or moss/seed (see pages 38–39).

The length of the skirt can be varied according to taste, but the fit across the hips and up towards the waist must be precise. To help the skirt fit snugly around the waist a piece of ribbon elastic could be encased at the top of the skirt to create a waistband.

How to design and knit a straight skirt

Back panel

1 Calculate the number of stitches you need to cast on for the width of the skirt at the bottom edge (A). This should be wider than the measurement at the hip-line (C) to ensure ease of movement.

2 Calculate the number of stitches you need for the width of the skirt at the hipline (C).

3 Calculate the number of stitches you need for the width of the skirt at the waistline (D).

4 Calculate the number of rows you need to knit for the length of the skirt (E), beginning after the welt and finishing at the dotted line as indicated on the spec.

5 Calculate the number of rows you need to knit for the short straight section between the dotted line and the top of the skirt (J). (J should measure approximately 2.5 cm (1 in).)

6 Calculate the number of rows you need to knit to achieve the desired length (F), between (A) and (B), beginning after the welt. This section should be knitted straight without any shaping.

7 Calculate the number of rows you need to achieve the desired length (G), between (B) and (C).

8 Calculate the number of rows you need to knit for the desired length (H), between (C) and the dotted line.

9 Work out the number of paired decreases (see pages 70–71) needed to shape the side edges up to the hipline (G) between (B) and (C), and the number of paired decreases needed to shape the side edges up to the waistline (H) between (C) and the dotted line. The decreases between (B) and (C) should be shaped gradually, with the decreases spaced closer together towards the hipline. This will help to create a smooth curve around the hips. Use proportional graph paper if necessary to help you work out the decreases.

10 Cast/bind off the remaining stitches (D) loosely. (At this point a hem could be knitted if desired to encase a piece of ribbon elastic. This would help fit the skirt around the waist.)

Front panel

11 The front panel is knitted the same as the back panel.

How to join the panels

12 Join the back and front side seams.

13 A piece of elastic ribbon could be sewn into the inside of the skirt at the top edge if desired.

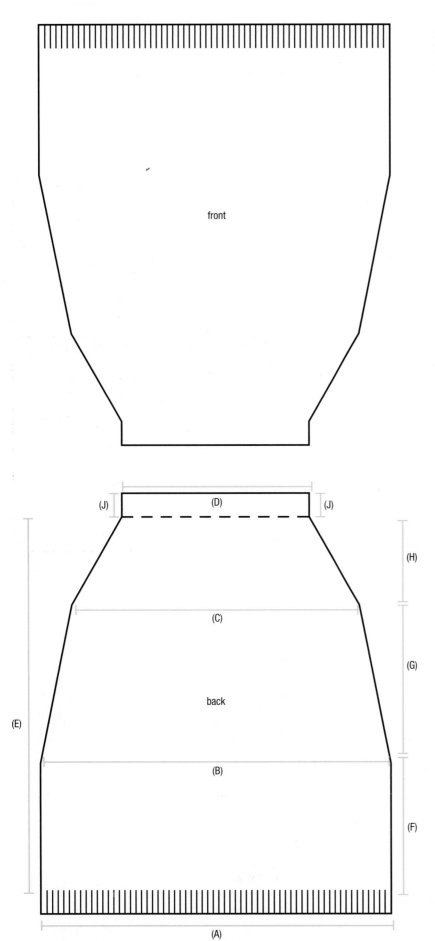

It is best to knit a skirt to a firm tension/gauge using a hard-wearing yarn so that the skirt doesn't 'bag' when it is worn.

front

(J) (D) (J)

(H)

(C)

(G)

back

(E)

(B)

(F)

(A)

Basic necklines

The neck shaping on a garment can be designed to suit individual tastes, but it should also complement the style of the garment.

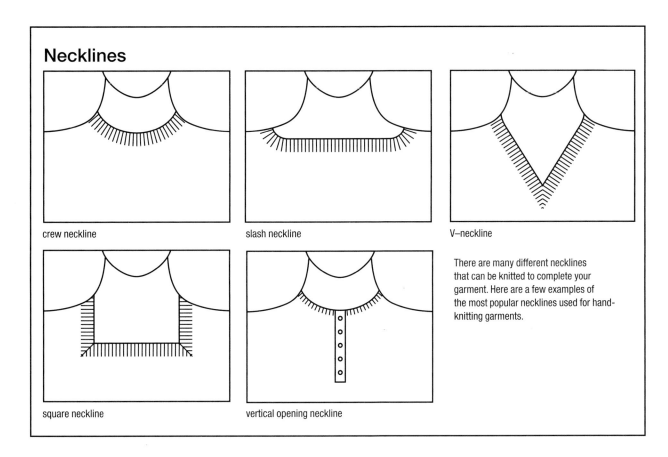

Necklines

crew neckline

slash neckline

V–neckline

square neckline

vertical opening neckline

There are many different necklines that can be knitted to complete your garment. Here are a few examples of the most popular necklines used for hand-knitting garments.

The shape of the neckline should be planned onto your spec drawing with measurements so that you can calculate how it is to be knitted. Usually it is easier to work this out on proportional graph paper, although formulas can also be used.

The back neck is usually either left unshaped and cast/bind off straight, or it is dipped down slightly at each edge to give it a better shape.

Many necklines are finished off with a band that is either picked up or knitted separately and sewn on. It is important to consider the depth of the band when deciding on the width and depth of the neckline, as this will decrease the total circumference. If you want to add a collar, turn to pages 118–119).

Crew neckline

This is a classic round neckline that creates a half-circle at the front.

1 The depth of the front neck drop should be no less than 7 cm (2¾ in), and the width of the back neck should be no less than 15 cm (6 in) for a woman or 16 cm (6¼ in) for a man (see sizing charts on pages 121–124). Remember that on a sweater, if these measurements are too short, there might not be enough room for the head to pass through the garment.

2 Calculate the number of stitches you need for the desired width of the back neck.

3 Calculate the number of rows you need to knit to achieve the desired depth of the front neck.

4 Work to the beginning of the front neck shaping, and put approximately one third of the stitches on a holder at the centre front (or cast them off).

5 Subtract the number of stitches at the centre front from the number of stitches for the back neck to give you the number of decreases needed to shape the neck. This must be an even number. Divide this number in half because there will be an equal number of decreases worked at each side of the front neck.

6 Work out the shaping for one side of the neck and then it can be reversed to shape the other side. Create a smooth curve by decreasing stitches at each end of every row, then at each end of every other row until the correct number of stitches has been decreased. Then work the remaining rows straight.

7 Draw the neckline onto proportional graph paper to make sure that the curve is smooth (see page 69). If it looks too angular, you might have to alter the number of stitches at the centre front and re-draw the decreases.

Slash neckline

This neckline has a wide opening and minimal shaping.

1 The width of the back neck can be 20–30 cm (7¾–11¾ in), depending on the body width across the shoulders and whether or not you want the garment to sit on the shoulders or hang off them.

2 Calculate the number of stitches you need for the desired width of the back neck.

3 Calculate the number of rows you need to knit to achieve the desired depth of the front neck. This only needs to be a short drop (approximately 3 cm (1¼ in)). Alternatively, the front neck can be cast/bind off straight without any shaping.

4 Work to the beginning of the front neck shaping and put almost all of the stitches for the front neck on a holder, leaving approximately 4 cm (1½ in) of stitches at each side for shaping (unless the stitches are going to be cast/bind off straight).

5 Subtract the number of stitches at the centre front from the number of stitches for the back neck to give you the number of decreases needed to shape the neck. This must be an even number. Divide this number in half because there will be an equal number of decreases worked at each side of the front neck.

6 Work out the shaping for one side of the neck and then it can be reversed to shape the other side. Create a smooth curve by decreasing stitches at each end of every row, then at each end of every other row until the correct number of stitches has been decreased. Then work the remaining rows straight.

7 Draw the neckline onto proportional graph paper to make sure that the curve is smooth (see page 69). If it looks too angular, you might have to alter the number of stitches at the centre front and re-draw the decreases.

V-neckline

This type of neckline can be worked to any depth and to any angle.

1 The degree of the angle is determined by the frequency of decreases along the neck edge. For example, if the decreases are spaced closely together this will create a wide angle, but if they are spaced further apart this will create a narrower shape.

2 It doesn't matter whether the body panel has an odd or even number of stitches before the V-neck shaping. If the body panel has an odd number of stitches, the central stitch is left on a holder and becomes the axial stitch of the band. If the garment has an even number of stitches, the bar between the centre two stitches is picked up and this becomes the axial stitch for the band.

3 Calculate the number of stitches you need for the desired width of the back neck.

4 Calculate how many rows you need to knit to achieve the desired depth of the V-neck.

5 Work to the beginning of the front neck shaping and divide the number of stitches for the back neck in half. This will give you the number of decreases that you need to make at each side of the neck.

6 Work out the number of paired decreases needed to shape the V-neck (see pages 70–71), making sure that you finish with several straight rows at the top after the decreases have been completed.

Picking up stitches

When stitches are picked up around a neckline, they must be picked up evenly to ensure that the band lays flat. So, pick up every stitch when you are picking up across stitches. When you are picking up across rows, pick up three out of four stitches.

This formula can be used for picking up stitches around any edge, including cardigan/jacket fronts, armholes, pocket tops, sock heels and blankets.

7 Draw the neckline onto proportional graph paper to make sure that the angle is smooth. If the decreases are not working out correctly, you might have to alter the depth of the neckline and/or the number of stitches in the back neck and re-draw the decreases.

Square neckline

This is one of the easiest necklines to knit because it has no decreases to work out for the shaping. Instead, stitches are simply cast/bind off at the beginning of the front neck drop and then the neck is worked straight to the shoulders. The band for a square neckline is, however, more complicated to knit than others because it has to be mitred.

1 Calculate the number of stitches you need for the desired width of the back neck.

2 Calculate how many rows you need to knit to achieve the desired depth of the front neck.

3 Work to the beginning of the front neck drop, and cast/bind off the centre stitches (same number as the back neck).

4 Work rows straight to the shoulder.

Vertical opening (a placket with buttons)

A vertical opening with a button fastening can give a sweater a completely different look, imitating the style of a shirt. The front opening needs to be planned out carefully onto the front panel to make sure that it is centred. The width of the button/buttonhole bands also needs to be considered and planned out so that the buttonholes sit exactly in the middle of the garment and not off to one side.

1 Follow the instructions for designing a crew neck (see page 115–116), and draw it out onto proportional graph paper. But do not begin to knit it until you have worked out the placket as follows.

2 Calculate how many rows down from the front neck drop you want the vertical opening to begin.

3 Decide on the number of stitches that you want for the width of the button/buttonhole bands.

4 Plan out the spacing of the buttonholes so that they fit evenly along the length of the vertical opening. (Buttonholes should be on the right-hand side for women and on the left-hand side for men.)

5 Work to the centre point of the front panel, and cast on half the number of stitches for the band. (Leave the remaining stitches for the right front on a holder.)

6 Work the stitches for the band in the firm stitch, such as rib, moss/seed or garter (see pages 38–39). These stitches will continue to be worked in a firm stitch for the entire length of the placket.

7 The placket for the right-hand side will be knitted to match the one on the left-hand side, casting on stitches as before at the centre front opening and working them in a firm stitch.

8 Draw out the positioning of the placket onto proportional graph paper so that you can see where the top of the placket hits the beginning of the crew neck shaping. The top of the placket should meet the neckline with the middle of the bands hitting the middle of the centre stitches at the beginning of the front neck drop. When the neckline is shaped, the extra stitches for the band on each side of the opening will be included in the centre stitches that are cast/bind off.

Basic collars

There are endless collar variations that can be experimented with to finish off a neckline as an alternative to a knitted band.

Collars are influenced by the width, shape and depth of the neckline to which they are to be attached, so each one needs to be designed individually for a perfect fit.

Stitches are either picked up around the neckline, or the collar is knitted as a separate panel and sewn on. If the collar is knitted separately the number of stitches for the width has to be calculated carefully and then it has to be sewn onto the neckline so that it sits evenly around the circumference.

The cast-on edge can be either the outer edge of the collar or the edge that meets the neckline. However, if the stitches for the collar are picked up, the collar is worked in one direction only – from the neckline to the outer edge.

Advice on six basic collars is given here, all of which can be adapted and developed further if desired.

Straight collar

This is the most basic collar and it is used with round necklines. A short collar of limited depth (no more than 7.5 cm (3 in)) can be knitted as a straight panel. However, a longer collar will need to be slightly shaped so that it is wider at the outer edge than it is at the neck edge.

This shaping can be done very easily without the need for decreasing. If the collar is knitted from the outer edge towards the neckline, simply change to a smaller size needle about half way along the length of it. If the collar is knitted from the neckline down to the outer edge, begin with a smaller needle and change to a larger needle.

Eton collar

This is knitted in a similar way to the straight collar, but the edges of it are shaped on each side to create more exaggerated points. The frequency of shaping is determined by how pointed you want the collar to be. If you shape the edges on every row, the points will look more severe, whereas less frequent shaping will create a softer angle to the collar.

If the collar is knitted from the outer edge towards the neckline, the edges will need to be decreased. If the collar is knitted from the neckline down to the outer edge, the edges will need to be increased.

Classic roll neck

This is used with a shallow, round neckline to create a soft roll of fabric around the neck; it is also often referred to as a 'polo neck'. It is created by either knitting a separate rectangular piece of fabric that is sewn to the neckline with a seam at the shoulder point, or by picking up stitches around the neck and knitting a cylindrical tube on circular or double-pointed needles, which eliminates the seam.

The collar should be knitted to twice the length of its desired depth because the roll double backs on itself to create a double layer of fabric. Therefore, the

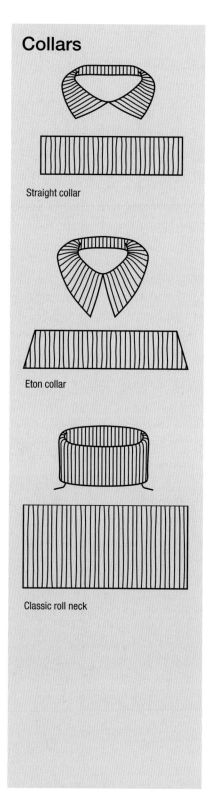

Collars

Straight collar

Eton collar

Classic roll neck

length of the wearer's neck should be considered to ensure that the roll sits comfortably around the neck and not over the chin.

Cowl collar

This is knitted in a similar way to a classic roll, but the length of the roll is considerably longer so that it creates a lot of extra fabric which folds over loosely around the neck. The neckline is wider and deeper than a classic round neck so make the width of the collar itself greater, too.

Basic shawl collar for a sweater

This type of collar is set into a square neckline and it rolls back on itself to create a soft, curved edge around the neck.

The collar is knitted as a separate rectangular panel which is joined to the horizontal front edge with both ends of the row-end edges sewn on top of each other. This means that the number of rows knitted for the collar must match the width of the square neckline so that the two pieces fit together perfectly.

The width of the collar should also be considered carefully so that enough stitches are cast on to match the circumference of the neckline (minus the horizontal front edge).

Basic shawl collar for a cardigan

A shawl collar for a cardigan can be knitted either vertically or horizontally, depending on the pattern and desired way of working. It is created by knitting an elliptical shape as a separate panel that is then attached to a V-neckline.

It is best to attach the curved edge of the collar to the neckline so that the neater, straight edge is the outer one. This means that the length of the curved edge must be designed to match the circumference of the neckline that it is being sewn to. It is crucial that these two edges match each other precisely, so it might be wise to work out the shape of the curve on proportional graph paper before you attempt to knit it.

The depth of the collar is determined by the degree of shaping along the curved edge, and for a deeper collar more shaping is required to enable it to turn back comfortably and sit neatly on the shoulders.

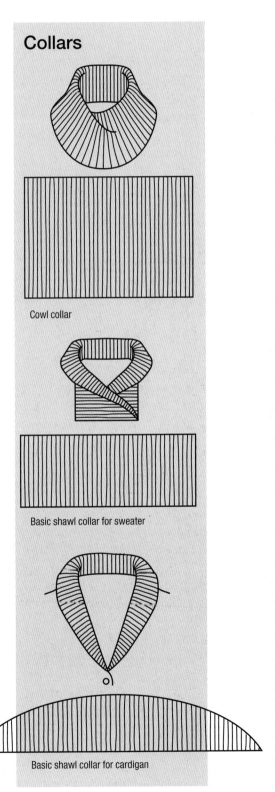

Collars

Cowl collar

Basic shawl collar for sweater

Basic shawl collar for cardigan

Advice on garments

There are some general points to consider about basic garment shapes.

• A welt in a firm stitch should be knitted after casting on the front, back and sleeve panels to stabilize the edges and stop them from curling (unless the edges are intended to be loose).

• The depth of the welt should be indicated on the spec, but it should not be included in the row calculation for the length of the garment. This is because it will probably be a different tension/gauge to the main knitting. Knit the welt to the desired depth and then subtract this depth from the total length of the garment.

• An even number of rows should be completed before beginning the armhole shaping so that you begin the left-hand armhole shaping with the right-side of the work facing towards you.

• An even number of rows should be completed before beginning the shoulder shaping so that you begin the left-hand shoulder shaping with the right-side of the work facing towards you.

• The amount of steps in a shaped shoulder depends on the desired fit of the garment and the weight of yarn being used. The closer the fit and the finer the yarn, the greater number of steps are needed.

• If the number of stitches in each shoulder step cannot be divided equally, make sure that each successive step towards the neck has fewer stitches in it.

• The stitches for the shoulders can be shaped by short row shaping if preferred, and/or left on a holder, rather than casting them off.

• Make sure that the width of the back neck is wide enough for the head to pass through.

• The back neck can be slightly shaped if desired by casting off a small step at each side of the neck edge so that it is slightly dipped.

• The stitches for the back neck can be left on a holder if preferred, rather than casting them off.

• On the spec drawing for each garment shape, the sleeve is shown in position to the front and back panels so that you can see how the panels relate to one another. However, remember that when you are mapping out the panels on proportional graph paper, the sleeve must be drawn the same way up as the front and back (see page 68).

Women's sizing chart

Bust	81 cm 32 in	86 cm 34 in	91 cm 36 in	97 cm 38 in	102 cm 40 in	107 cm 42 in	112 cm 44 in	117 cm 46 in	122 cm 48 in
Centre back neck to waist	40 cm 15¾ in	42 cm 16½ in	43 cm 17 in	44 cm 17¼ in	44 cm 17 in	45 cm 17¾ in	45 cm 17¾ in	46 cm 18 in	46 cm 18 in
Back (sweater or cardigan)	33 cm 13 in	34 cm 13½ in	35 cm 13¾ in	36 cm 14¼ in	37 cm 14½ in	38 cm 15 in	39 cm 15¼ in	40 cm 15¾ in	41 cm 16¼ in
Back (slipover)	31 cm 12¼ in	32 cm 12½ in	33 cm 13 in	34 cm 13½ in	35 cm 13¾ in	36 cm 14¼ in	37 cm 14½ in	38 cm 15 in	39 cm 15¼ in
Armhole (raglan sweater)	21 cm 8¼ in	22 cm 8¾ in	23 cm 9 in	24 cm 9½ in	25 cm 9¾ in	26 cm 10¼ in	27 cm 10¾ in	28 cm 11 in	29 cm 11½ in
Armhole (raglan cardigan)	22 cm 8¾ in	23 cm 9 in	24 cm 9½ in	25 cm 9¾ in	26 cm 10¼ in	27 cm 10¾ in	28 cm 11 in	29 cm 11½ in	30 cm 11¾ in
Armhole (drop or set-in sweater)	20 cm 7¾ in	20 cm 7¾ in	21 cm 8¼ in	21 cm 8¼ in	22 cm 8¾ in	22 cm 8¾ in	23 cm 9 in	23 cm 9 in	24 cm 9½ in
Armhole (drop or set-in cardigan)	21 cm 8¼ in	21 cm 8¼ in	22 cm 8¾ in	22 cm 8¾ in	23 cm 9 in	23 cm 9 in	24 cm 9½ in	24 cm 9½ in	25 cm 9¾ in
Sleeve seam (raglan or set-in)	43 cm 17 in	43 cm 17 in	44 cm 17¼ in	44 cm 17¼ in	45 cm 17¼ in	45 cm 17¾ in	45 cm 17¾ in	45 cm 17¾ in	45 cm 17¾ in
Sleeve seam (drop or square set-in)	46 cm 18 in	46 cm 18 in	47 cm 18½ in	47 cm 18½ in	47 cm 18½ in	48 cm 19 in	48 cm 19 in	48 cm 19 in	48 cm 19 in
Fitted sweater length	50 cm 19¾ in	52 cm 20½ in	53 cm 20¾ in	54 cm 21¼ in	54 cm 21¼ in	55 cm 21¾ in	55 cm 21¾ in	56 cm 22 in	56 cm 22 in
Wrist	21 cm 8¼ in	21 cm 8¼ in	22 cm 8¾ in	23 cm 9 in	23 cm 9 in	24 cm 9½ in	25 cm 9¾ in	25 cm 9¾ in	26 cm 10¼ in
Top arm (set-in sweater)	34 cm 13½ in	35 cm 13¾ in	36 cm 14¼ in	37 cm 14½ cm	38 cm 15 in	40 cm 15¾ in	41 cm 16¼ in	42 cm 16½ in	43 cm 17 in
Top arm (set-in cardigan)	35 cm 13¾ in	36 cm 14¼ in	37 cm 14½ in	38 cm 15 in	40 cm 15¾ in	41 cm 16¼ in	42 cm 16½ in	43 cm 17 in	44 cm 17¼ in
Top arm (raglan sweater)	38 cm 15 in	39 cm 15¼ in	40 cm 15¾ in	41 cm 16¼ in	42 cm 16½ in	44 cm 17¼ in	45 cm 17¾ in	46 cm 18 in	47 cm 18½ in
Top arm (raglan cardigan)	39 cm 15¼ in	40 cm 15¾ in	41 cm 16¼ in	42 cm 16½ in	44 cm 17¼ in	45 cm 17¾ in	46 cm 18 in	47 cm 18½ in	48 cm 19 in
Back neck	15 cm 6 in	16 cm 6¼ in	16 cm 6¼ in	17 cm 6¾ in	17 cm 6¾ in	17 cm 6¾ in	18 cm 7 in	18 cm 7 in	18 cm 7 in
Front neck	7 cm 2¾ in	7 cm 2¾ in	7 cm 2¾ in	8 cm 3¼ in	8 cm 3¼ in	8 cm 3¼ in	8 cm 3¼ in	8 cm 3¼ in	9 cm 3½ in
Hat (width all round head)	56 cm 22 in	56 cm 22 in	56 cm 22 in	56 cm 22 in	56 cm 22 in	56 cm 22 in	56 cm 22 in	56 cm 22 in	56 cm 22 in
Waist	60 cm 23½ in	65 cm 25½ in	70 cm 27½ in	75 cm 29½ in	80 cm 31½ in	85 cm 33½ in	90 cm 35½ in	95 cm 37½ in	100 cm 39½ in
Hips (18 cm (7 in) below the waist)	86 cm 33¾ in	91 cm 35¾ in	96 cm 37¾ in	102 cm 40¼ in	107 cm 42 in	112 cm 44 in	117 cm 46 in	122 cm 48 in	127 cm 50 in
Skirt length (to knee)	57 cm 22½ in	57 cm 22½ in	58 cm 22¾ in	59 cm 23¼ in	59 cm 23¼ in	60 cm 23½ in	60 cm 23½ in	61 cm 24 in	62 cm 24½ in

Men's sizing chart

Chest	86 cm 34 in	91 cm 36 in	97 cm 38 in	102 cm 40 in	107 cm 42 in	112 cm 44 in	117 cm 46 in	122 cm 48 in	127 cm 50 in
Back (sweater or cardigan)	35 cm 13¾ in	38 cm 15 in	39 cm 15¼ in	41 cm 16¼ in	42 cm 16½ in	44 cm 17¼ cm	45 cm 17¾ in	46 cm 18 in	48 cm 19 in
Back (slipover)	32 cm 12½ in	35 cm 13¾ in	36 cm 14¼ in	38 cm 15 in	39 cm 15¼ in	41 cm 16¼ in	42 cm 16½ in	43 cm 17 in	45 cm 17¾ in
Armhole (raglan sweater)	23 cm 9 in	24 cm 9½ in	25 cm 9¾ in	27 in 10¾ in	28 cm 11 in	29 cm 11½ in	30 cm 11¾ in	31 cm 12¼ in	32 cm 12½ in
Armhole (raglan cardigan)	24 cm 9½ in	25 cm 9¾ in	26 cm 10¼ in	28 cm 11 in	29 cm 11½ in	30 cm 11¾ in	31 cm 12¼ in	32 cm 12½ in	33 cm 13 in
Armhole (set-in sweater)	22 cm 8¾ in	23 cm 9 in	24 cm 9½ in	26 cm 10⅛ in	27 cm 10¾ in	28 cm 11 in	29 cm 11½ in	30 cm 11¾ in	31 cm 12¼ in
Armhole (set-in cardigan)	23 cm 9 in	24 cm 9½ in	25 cm 9¾ in	27 cm 10¾ in	28 cm 11 in	29 cm 11½ in	30 cm 11¾ in	31 cm 12¼ in	32 cm 12½ in
Armhole (drop shoulder sweater)	21 cm 8¼ in	22 cm 8¾ in	22 cm 8¾ in	23 cm 9 in	23 cm 9 in	24 cm 9½ in	24 cm 9½ in	25 cm 9¾ in	25 cm 9¾ in
Armhole (drop shoulder cardigan)	22 cm 8¾ in	23 cm 9 in	23 cm 9 in	24 cm 9½ in	24 cm 9½ in	25 cm 9¾ in	25 cm 9¾ in	26 cm 10¼ in	26 cm 10¼ in
Sleeve seam (raglan or set-in)	44 cm 17¼ in	46 cm 18 in	46 cm 18 in	47 cm 18½ in	47 cm 18½ in	48 cm 19 in	48 cm 19 in	49 cm 19¼ in	49 cm 19¼ in
Sleeve seam (drop or square set-in)	47 cm 18½ in	48 cm 19 in	48 cm 19 in	49 cm 19¼ in	49 cm 19¼ in	50 cm 19¾ in	50 cm 19¾ in	51 cm 20 in	51 cm 20 in
Wrist	22 cm 8¾ in	23 cm 9 in	24 cm 9½ in	24 cm 9½ in	25 cm 9¾ in	26 cm 10¼ in	26 cm 10¼ in	27 cm 10¾ in	27 cm 10¾ in
Top arm (sweater)	37 cm 14½ in	39 cm 15¼ in	40 cm 15¾ in	42 cm 16½ in	43 cm 17 in	44 cm 17¼ in	44 cm 17¼ in	45 cm 17¾ in	46 cm 18 in
Top arm (cardigan)	38 cm 15 in	40 cm 15¾ in	41 cm 16¼ in	43 cm 17 in	44 cm 17¼ in	45 cm 17¾ in	45 cm 17¾ in	46 cm 18 in	47 cm 18½ in
Back neck	16 cm 6¼ in	17 cm 6¾ in	17 cm 6¾ in	18 cm 7 in	18 cm 7 in	19 cm 7½ in	20 cm 7¾ in	21 cm 8¼ in	22 cm 8¾ in
Front neck	7 cm 2¾ in	7 cm 2¾ in	7 cm 2¾ in	7 cm 2¾ in	8 cm 3¼ in	8 cm 3¼ in	9 cm 3½ in	9 cm 3½ in	9 cm 3½ in
Hat (width all round head)	56 cm 22 in	57 cm 22½ in	57 cm 22½ in	57 cm 22½ in	57 cm 22½ in	57 cm 22½ in	57 cm 22½ in	57 cm 22½ in	57 cm 22½ in

Children's sizing chart

Chest	2–3 yrs	4–5 yrs	6–7 yrs	8–9 yrs	10–11 yrs
	56 cm	61 cm	66 cm	71 cm	76 cm
	32 in	34 in	36 in	38 in	40 in
Centre back	27 cm	29 cm	33 cm	36 cm	38 cm
neck to waist	10¾ in	11½ in	13 in	14¼ in	15 in
Back (sweater	23 cm	25 cm	27 cm	30 cm	32 cm
or cardigan)	9 in	9¾ in	10¾ in	11¾ in	12½ in
Back	21 cm	23 cm	25 cm	28 cm	30 cm
(slipover)	8¼ in	9 in	9¾ in	11 in	11¾ in
Armhole	13 cm	14 cm	15 cm	16 cm	18 cm
(raglan sweater)	5 in	5½ in	6 in	6½ in	7 in
Armhole	14 cm	15 cm	16 cm	17 cm	19 cm
(raglan cardigan)	5½ in	6 in	6¼ in	6¾ in	7½ in
Armhole	11 cm	13 cm	14 cm	15 cm	17 cm
(set-in sweater)	4¼ in	5 in	5½ in	6 in	6¾ in
Armhole	12 cm	14 cm	15 cm	16 cm	18 cm
(set-in cardigan)	4¾ in	5½ in	6 in	6¼ in	7 in
Armhole (drop or	13 cm	14 cm	15 cm	16 cm	17 cm
square set-in sweater)	5 in	5½ in	6 in	6¼ in	6¾ in
Armhole (drop or	14 cm	15 cm	16 cm	17 cm	18 cm
square set-in cardigan)	5½ in	6 in	6¼ in	6¾ in	7 in
Sleeve seam (raglan	23 cm	27 cm	31 cm	35 cm	39 cm
or set-in)	9 in	10¾ in	12¼ in	13¾ in	15¼ in
Sleeve seam (drop	26 cm	30 cm	34 cm	38 cm	42 cm
or square set-in)	10¼ in	11¾ in	13½ in	15 in	16½ in
Average sweater	33 cm	38 cm	42 cm	46 cm	49 cm
length	13 in	15 in	16½ in	18 in	19¼ in
Wrist	15 cm	16 cm	17 cm	18 cm	19 cm
	6 in	6¼ in	6¾ in	7 in	7½ in
Top arm (sweater)	24 cm	25 cm	27 cm	28 cm	30 cm
	9½ in	9¾ in	10¾ in	11 in	11¾ in
Top arm (cardigan)	25 cm	27 cm	28 cm	30 cm	32 cm
	9¾ in	10¾ in	11 in	11¾ in	12½ in
Back neck	11 cm	11 cm	12 cm	13 cm	14 cm
	4¼ in	4¼ in	4¾ in	5 in	5½ in
Front neck	4 cm	4 cm	5 cm	5 cm	5 cm
	1½ in	1½ in	2 in	2 in	2 in
Hat (width all	47 cm	47 cm	49 cm	52 cm	52 cm
round head)	18½ in	18½ in	19¼ in	20½	20½ in

Babies' sizing chart

	3–5lb	5–7lbs	0–6 mths	6–12 mths	1–2 yrs
Chest	31 cm 12 in	36 cm 14 in	41 cm 16 in	46 cm 18 in	51 cm 20 in
Centre back neck to waist	12 cm 4¾ in	13 cm 5 in	16 cm 6¼ in	19 cm 7½ in	23 cm 9 in
Back (sweater or cardigan)	13 cm 5 in	15 cm 6 in	16 cm 6¼ in	18 cm 7 in	20 cm 7¾ in
Back (slipover)	11 cm 4¼ in	13 cm 5 in	14 cm 5½ in	16 cm 6¼ in	18 cm 7 in
Armhole (raglan sweater)	6 cm 2¼ in	8 cm 3¼ in	10 cm 4 in	11 cm 4¼ in	12 cm 4¾ in
Armhole (raglan cardigan)	7 cm 2¾ in	9 cm 3½ in	11 cm 4¼ in	12 cm 4¾ in	14 cm 5 in
Armhole (set-in sweater)	5 cm 2 in	7 cm 2¾ in	9 cm 3½ in	10 cm 4 in	10 cm 4 in
Armhole (set-in cardigan)	6 cm 2¼ in	8 cm 3¼ in	10 cm 4 in	11 cm 4¼ in	11 cm 4¼ in
Armhole (drop or square set-in sweater)	6 cm 2¼ in	8 cm 3¼ in	10 cm 4 in	11 cm 4¼ in	12 cm 4¾ in
Armhole (drop or square set-in cardigan)	7 cm 2¾ in	9 cm 3½ in	11 cm 4¼ in	12 cm 4¾ in	13 cm 5 in
Sleeve seam (raglan or set-in)	9 cm 3½ in	11 cm 4¼ in	12 cm 4¾ in	15 cm 6 in	19 cm 7½ in
Sleeve seam (drop or square set-in)	10 cm 4 in	12 cm 4¾ in	13 cm 5 in	16 cm 6¼ in	20 cm 7¾ in
Average sweater length	15 cm 6 in	17 cm 6¾ in	21 cm 8¼ in	24 cm 9½ in	29 cm 11½ in
Wrist	8 cm 3¼ in	10 cm 4 in	11 cm 4¼ in	13 cm 5 in	14 cm 5½ in
Top arm (sweater)	13 cm 5 in	15 cm 6 in	18 cm 7 in	21 cm 8¼ in	22 cm 8¾ in
Top arm (cardigan)	14 cm 5½ in	16 cm 6¼ in	19 cm 7½ in	22 cm 8¾ in	23 cm 9 in
Back neck	6 cm 2¼ in	7 cm 2¾ in	8 cm 3¼ in	9 cm 3½ in	10 cm 4 in
Front neck	2 cm ¾ in	3 cm 1¼ in	3 cm 1¼ in	3 cm 1¼ in	4 cm 1½ in
Hat (width all round head)	28 cm 11 in	31 in 12¼ in	33 cm 13 in	36 cm 14¼ in	38 cm 15 in

Useful information

Abbreviations
This list contains standard abbreviations and you should use these when you are writing up your own knitting patterns (see page 81).

alt	alternate
beg	begin(ning)
cm	centimetre(s)
col	colour(way)
cont	continu(e)(ing)
c4b	cable four (or number stated) back
c4f	cable four (or number stated) forward
cr	cross
dec	decrease(e)(ing)
dp	double-pointed
foll(s)	follow(s)(ing)
g	gram(s)
g st	garter stitch
in	inch
inc	increas(e)(ing)
K	knit
k2tog	knit two stitches together
kw	knitwise
LH	left hand
m1	make 1
mb	make bobble
ml	make loop
mm	millimetre(s)
oz	ounce(s)
P	purl
p2tog	purl two stitches together
patt	pattern
PB	place bead
pnso	pass next stitch over
psso	pass slipped stitch over
pw	purlwise
rem	remain(ing)
rep(s)	repeat(s)
rev st st	reverse stocking/stockinette stitch
RH	right hand
RS	right side of work
skpo	slip1, knit 1, pass slipped stitch over
sl	slip
ssk	slip, slip, knit two stitches together
st(s)	stitch(es)
st st	stocking/stockinette stitch
tbl	through back of loop(s)
tog	together
t2b	twist two (or number stated) back
t2f	twist two (or number stated) forward
WS	wrong side of work.
wyb	with yarn at back
wyf	with yarn at front
yf	yarn forward
yo	yarn over
yon	yarn over needle
yrn	yarn round needle
*	repeat instructions between * as many times as instructed
[ ]	repeat instructions between [ ] as many times as instructed

Needle sizes

US size	Metric size	Canadian size
15	10	000
13	9	00
11	8	0
11	7½	1
10½	7	2
10½	6½	3
10	6	4
9	5½	5
8	5	6
7	4½	7
6	4	8
5	3¾	9
4	3½	–
3	3¼	10
2–3	3	11
2	2¾	12
1	2¼	13
0	2	14

UK and US knitting terminology
Most terms used in UK and US knitting patterns are the same, but a few are different. The most common differences are listed here:

UK	US	UK	US
cast off	bind off	yarn over needle	yarn over (yo)
moss stitch	seed stitch	yarn forward	yarn over (yo)
stocking stitch	stockinette stitch	yarn round needle	yarn over (yo)
tension	gauge		

Index

Acknowledgements

I would like to thank the following people who worked enthusiastically with me on this project and made it happen: Katy Denny for offering me the initial idea and giving me the opportunity to fulfil it, Ruth Hamilton for her wonderful editorial skills and continuous support and guidance throughout, Kate Haxell for copy editing the book with such wonderful attention to detail, Colin Goody and Penny Stock for working so hard on the design of the book and making it look fabulous, Kang Chen for his fine illustrations and my dad, Tom Abrahams for letting me use his beautiful paintings.

Executive Editor Katy Denny

Project Editor Ruth Hamilton

Executive Art Editor Penny Stock

Designer Colin Goody

Copy Editor Kate Haxell

Senior Production Controller Martin Croshaw

Picture acknowledgements

All photos copyright Octopus Publishing Group. Vanessa Davies 2, 4 all, 8, 24, 25, 27, 30, 46, 58, 71, 76, 82, 88; Janine Hosegood 37 left, 37 right, 55, 78, 83, 90; Andy Komorowski cover, 16, 17, 18, 19, 20, 21, 22, 23, 28, 38, 48, 49, 52 above and below, 56, 57; Adrian Pope 15, 26, 64, 84; Gareth Sambidge 51; Joey Toller 65.

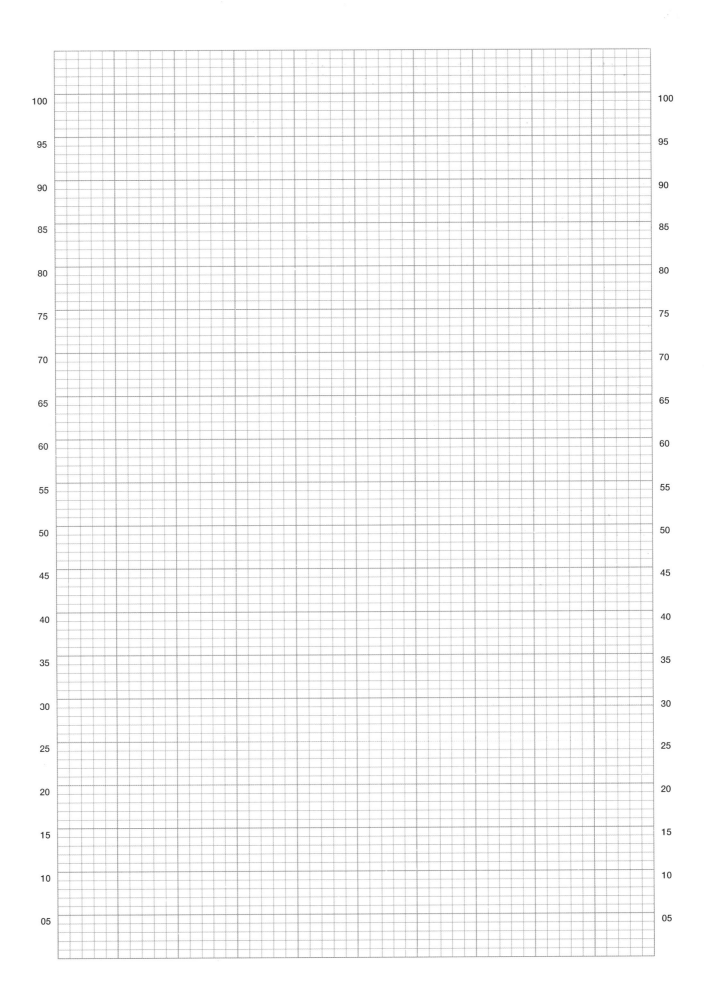

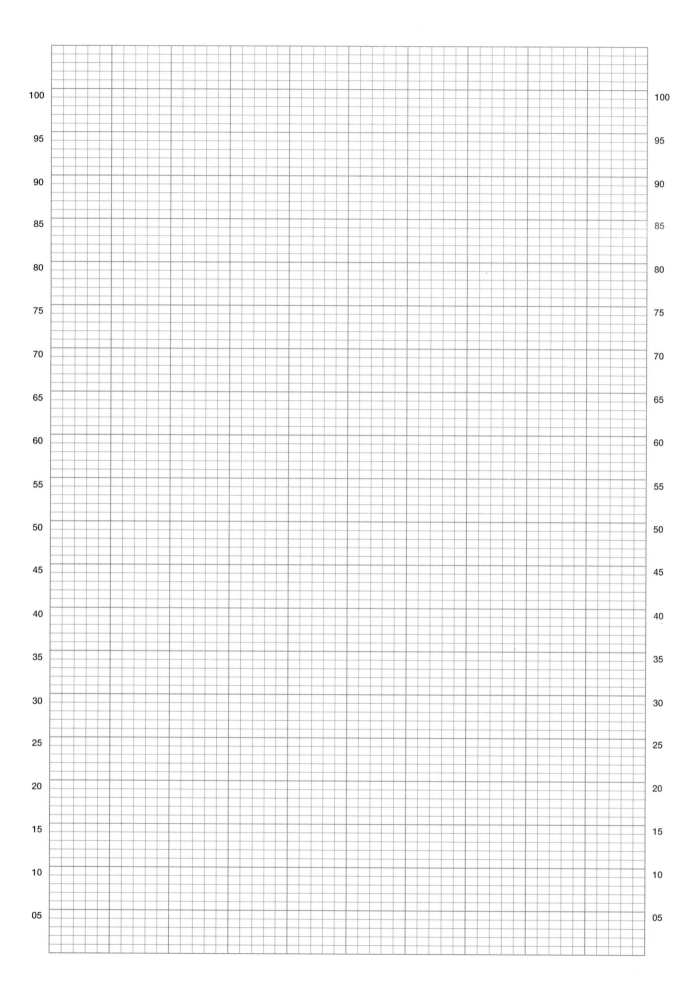

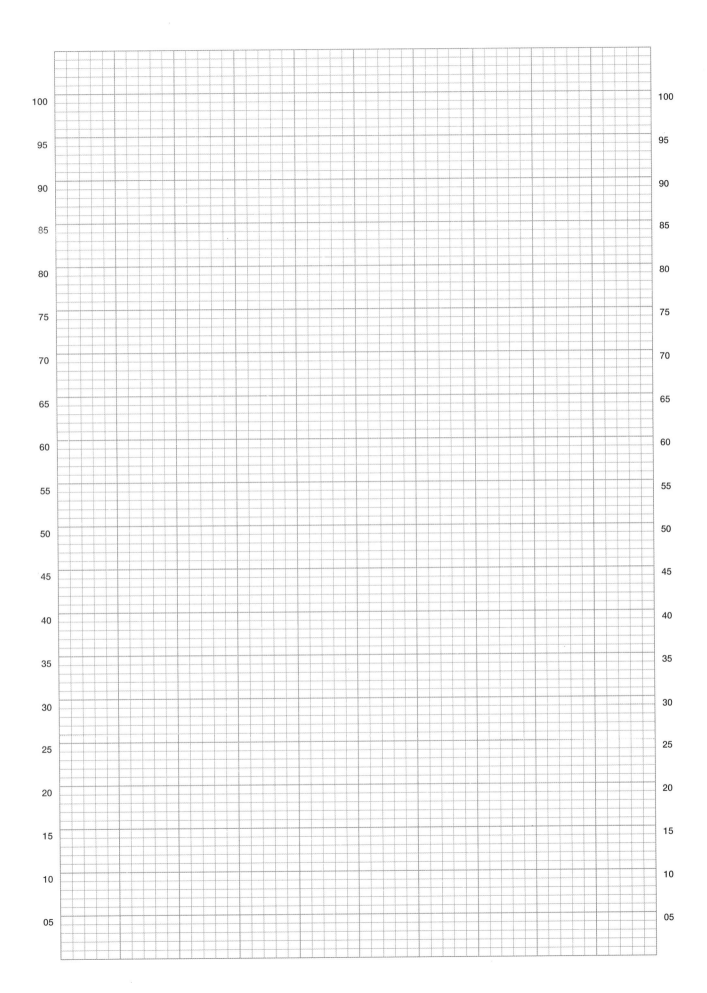

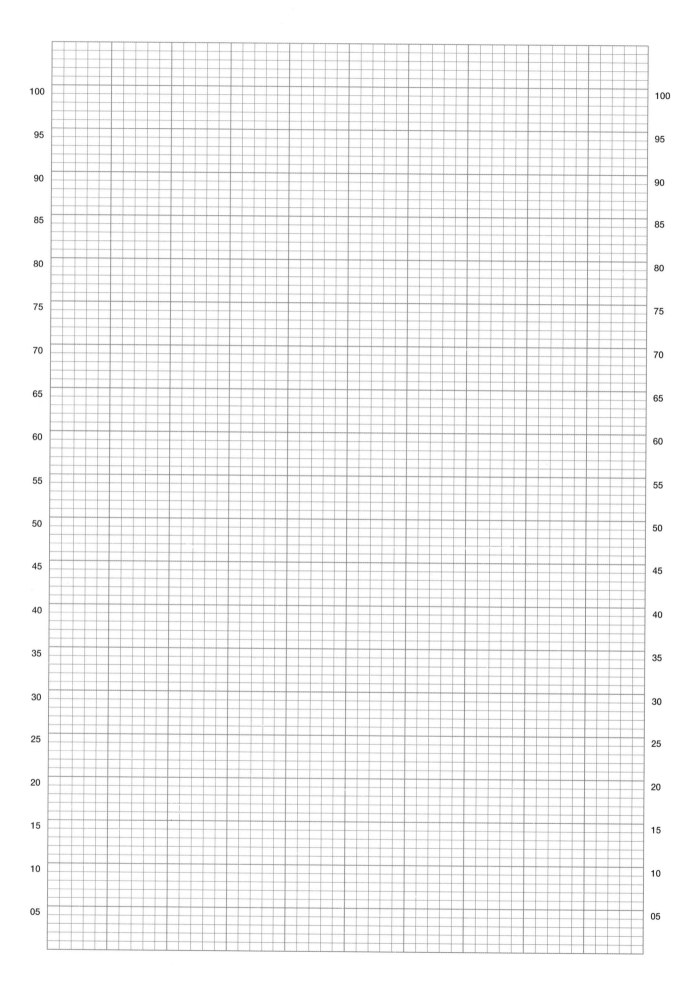

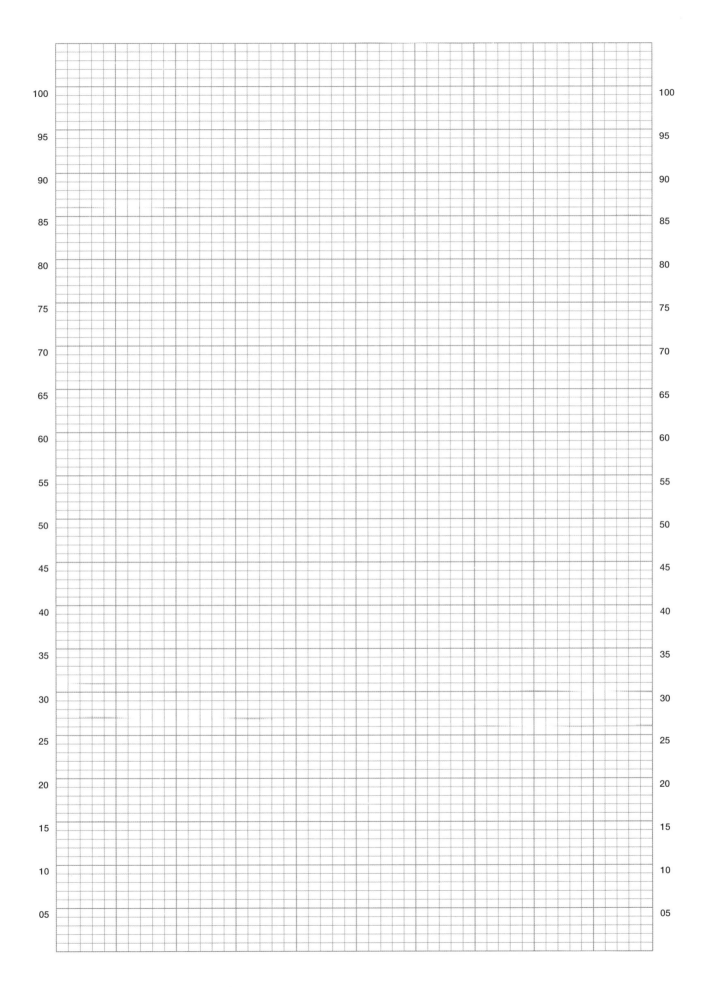

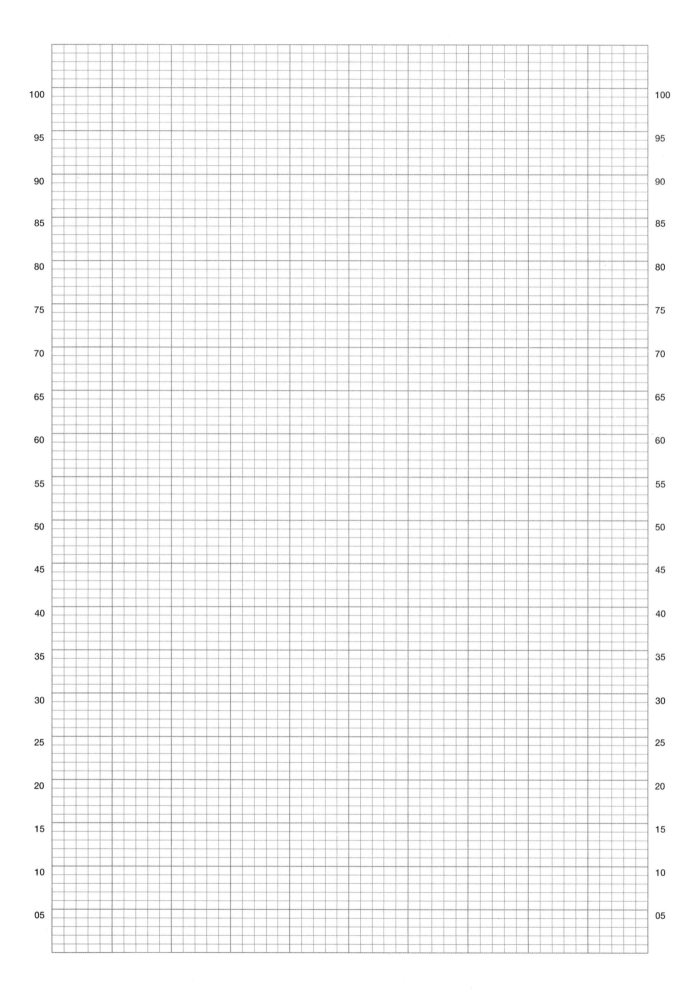

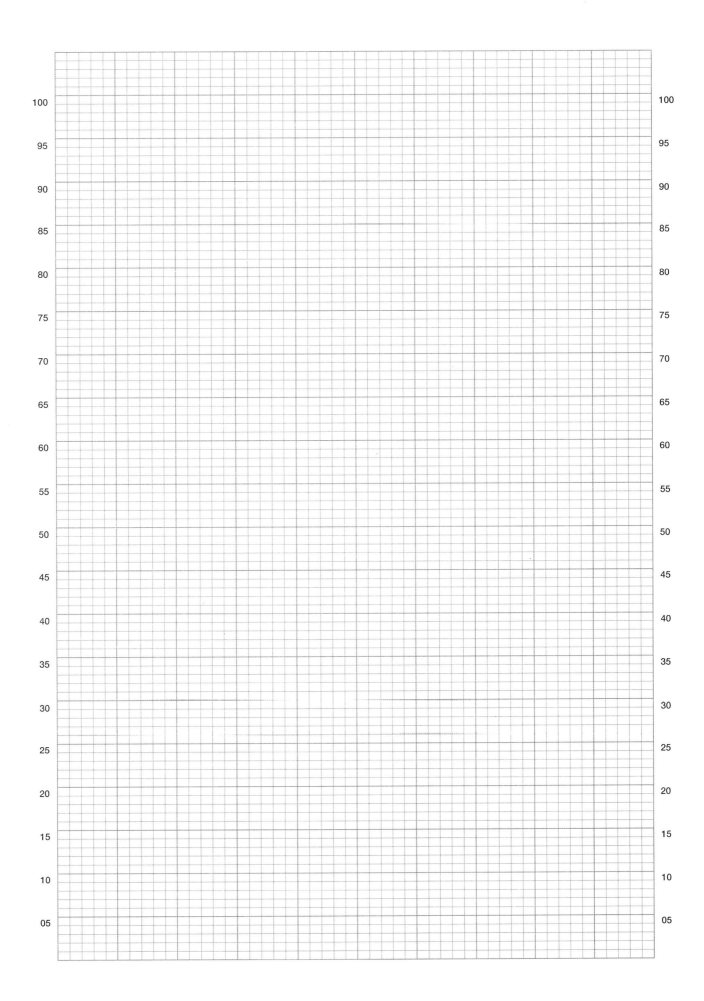

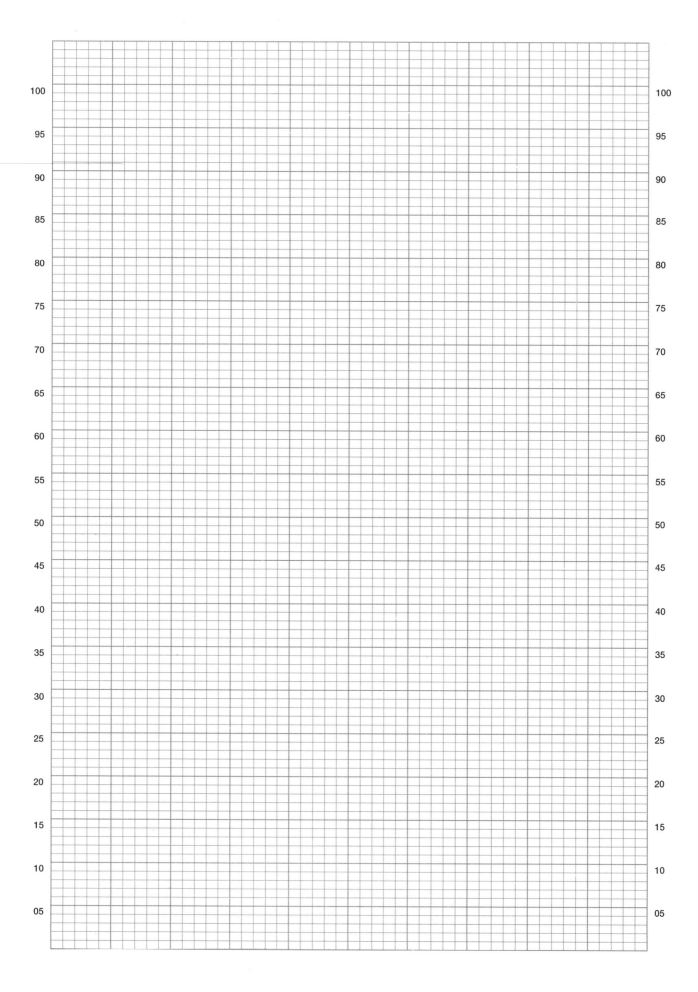

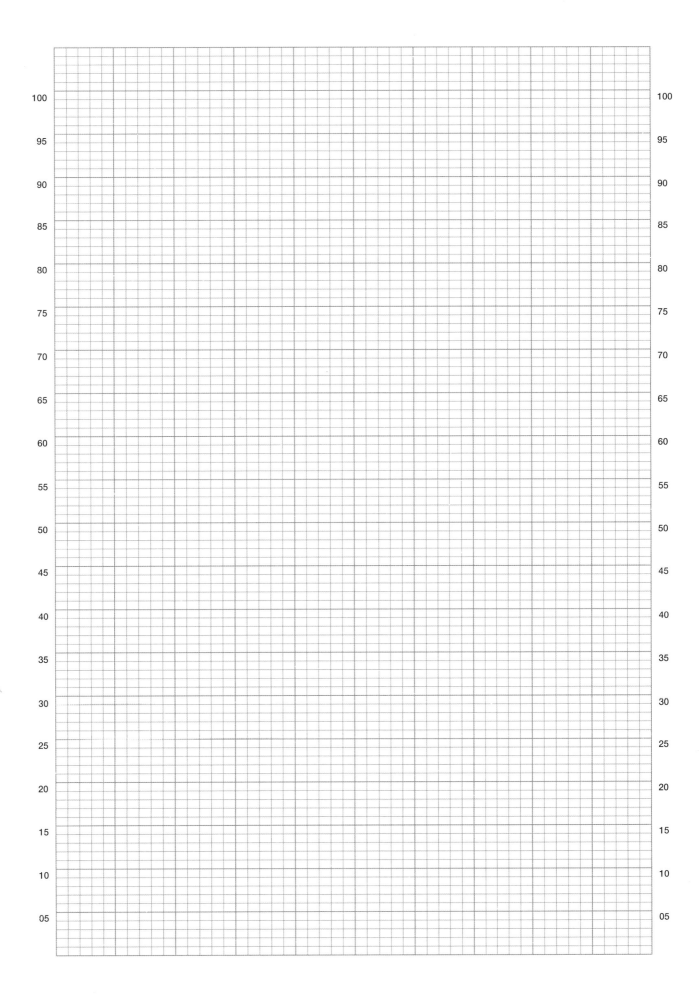

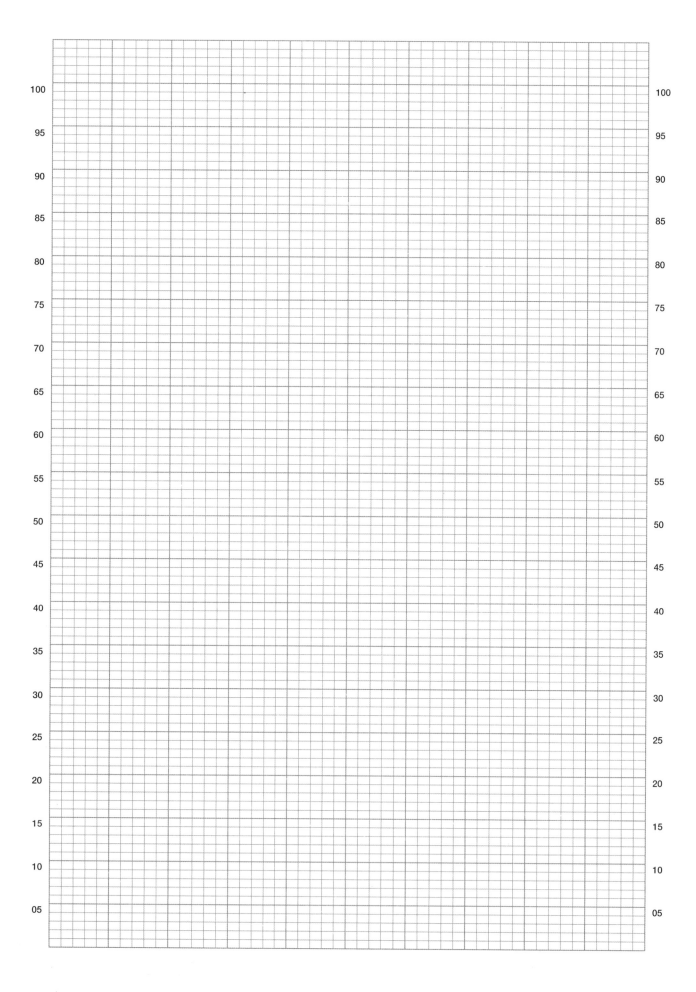

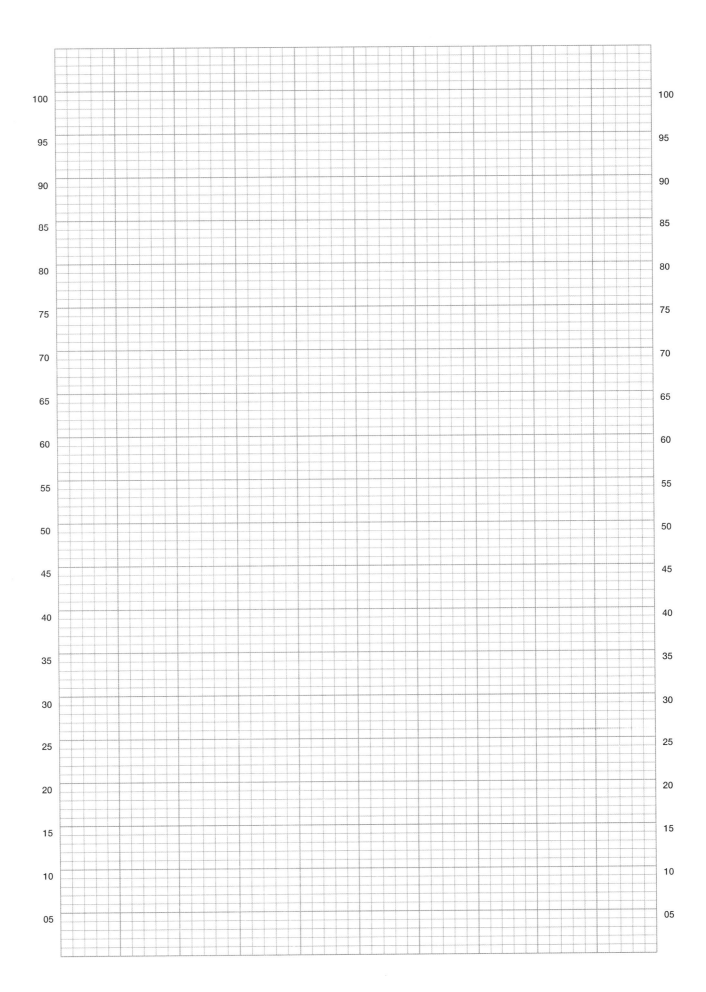

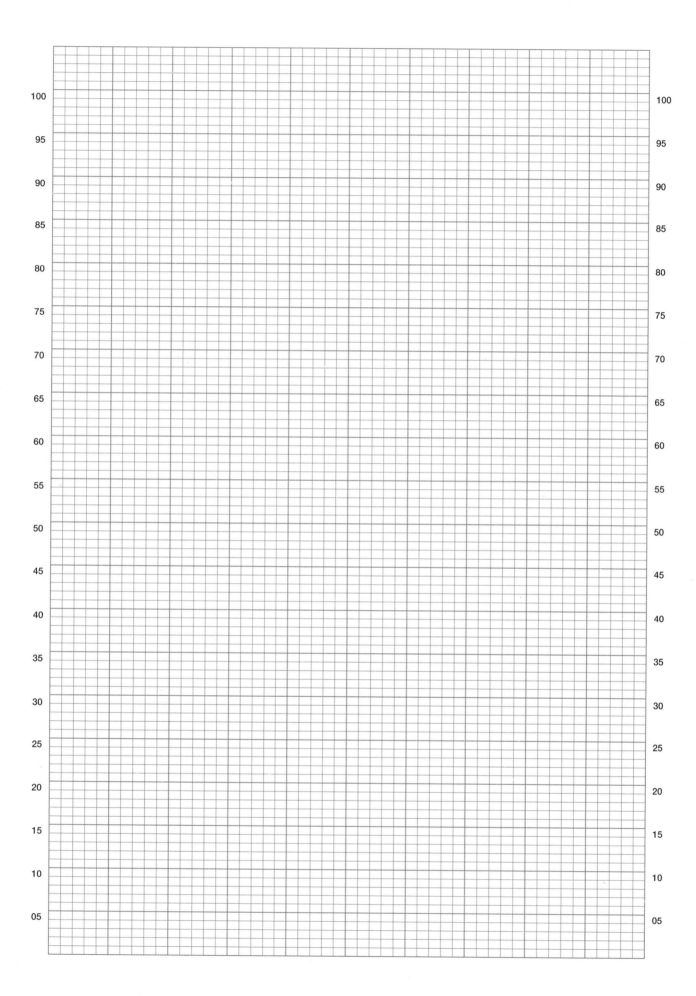

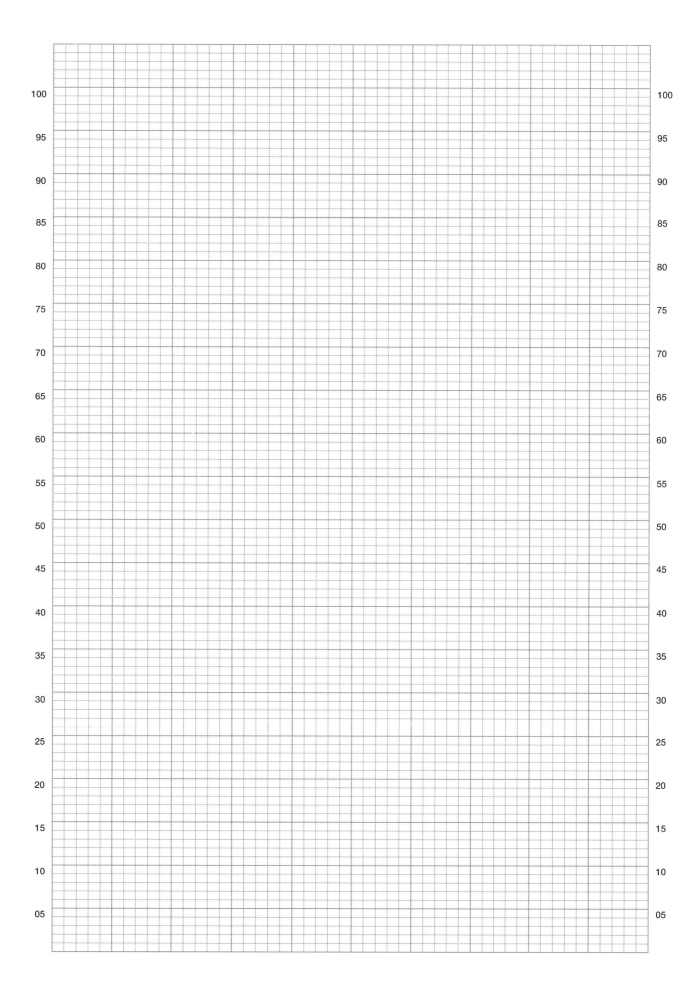

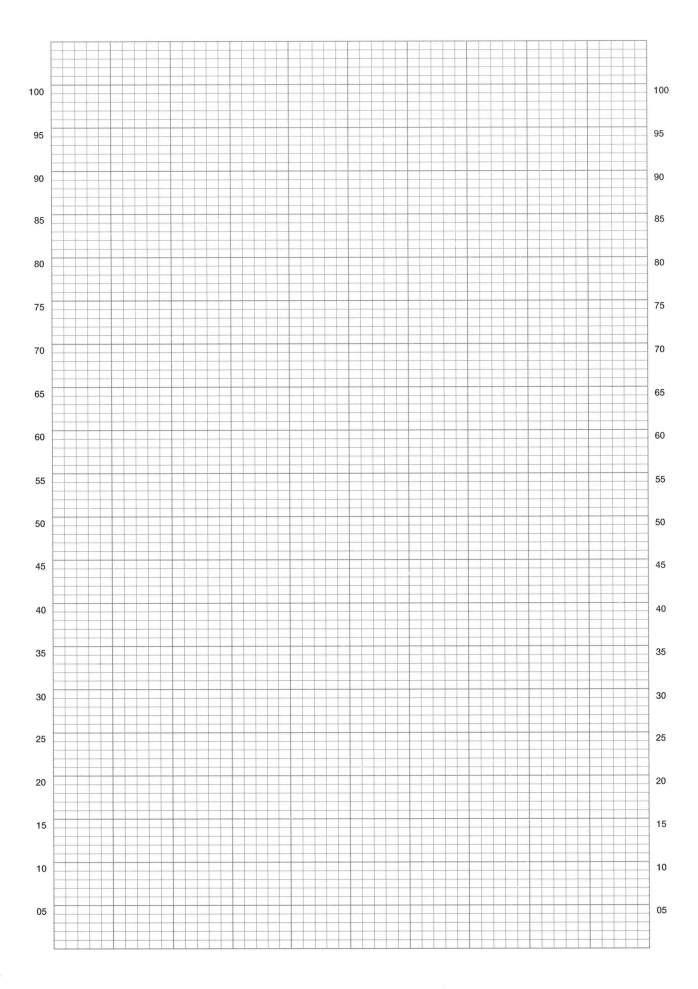

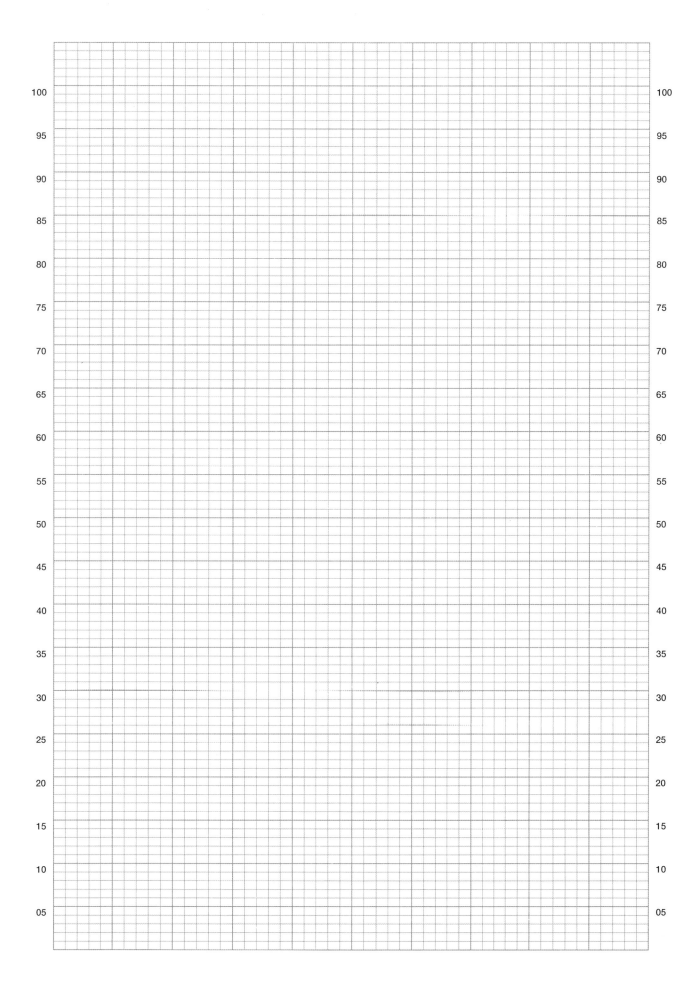

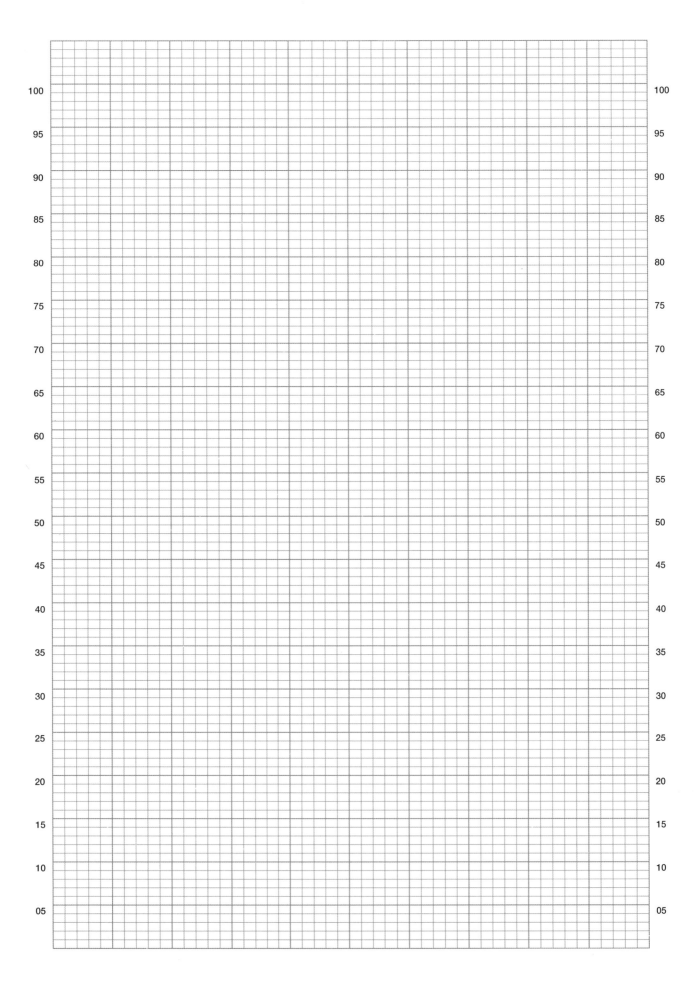

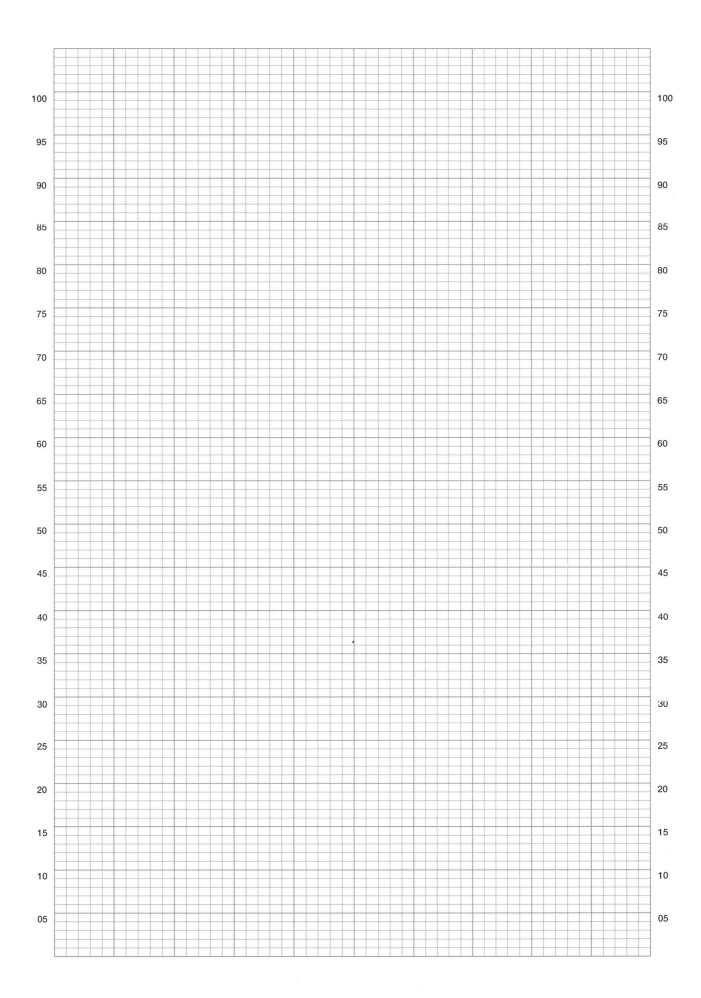

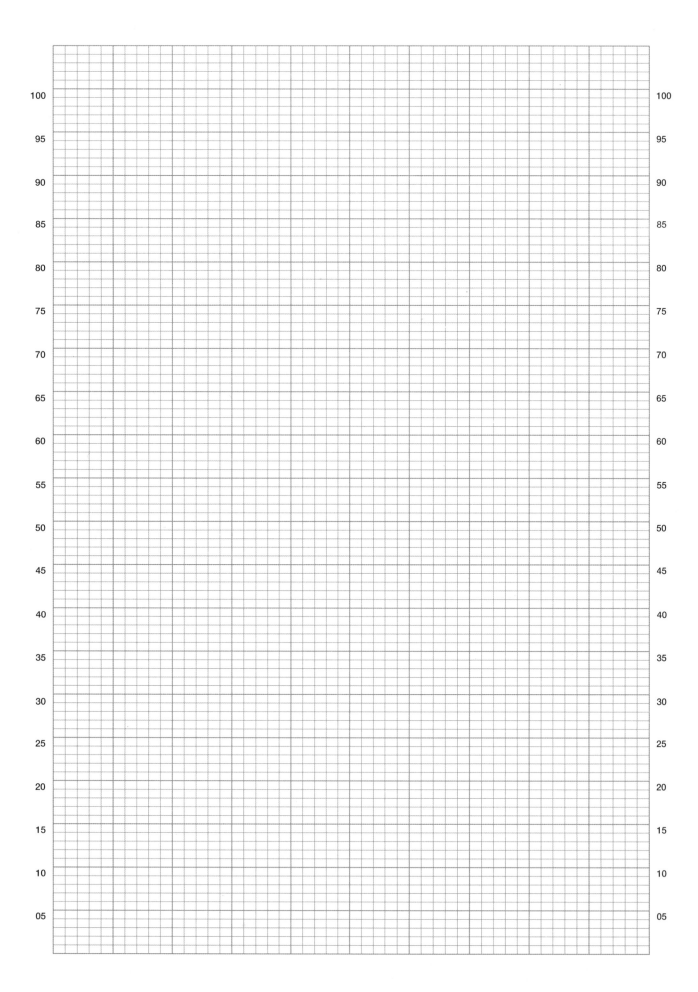

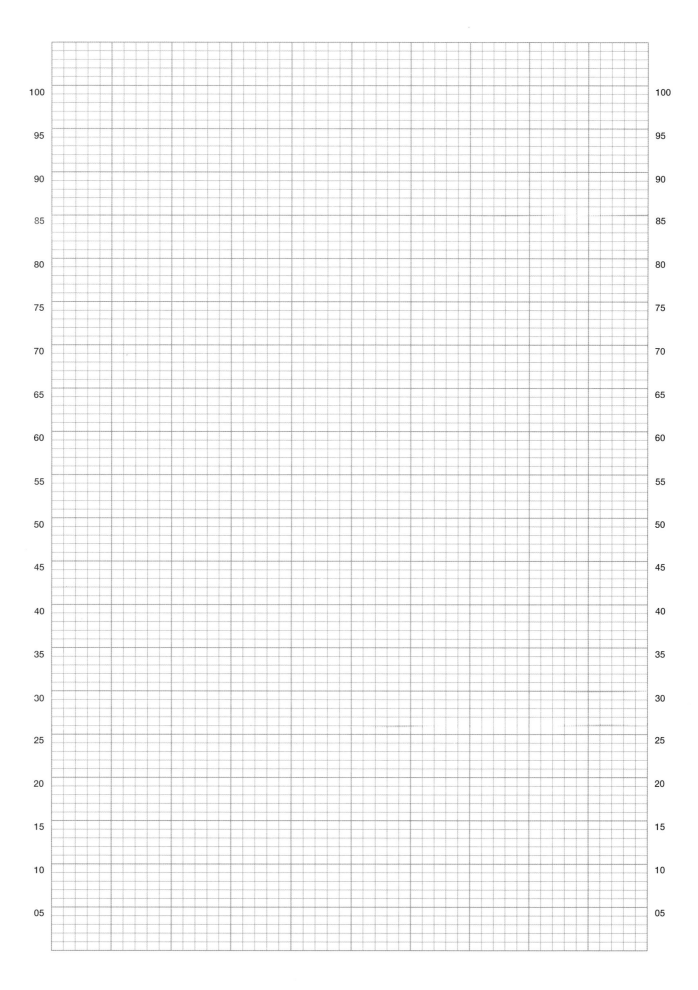

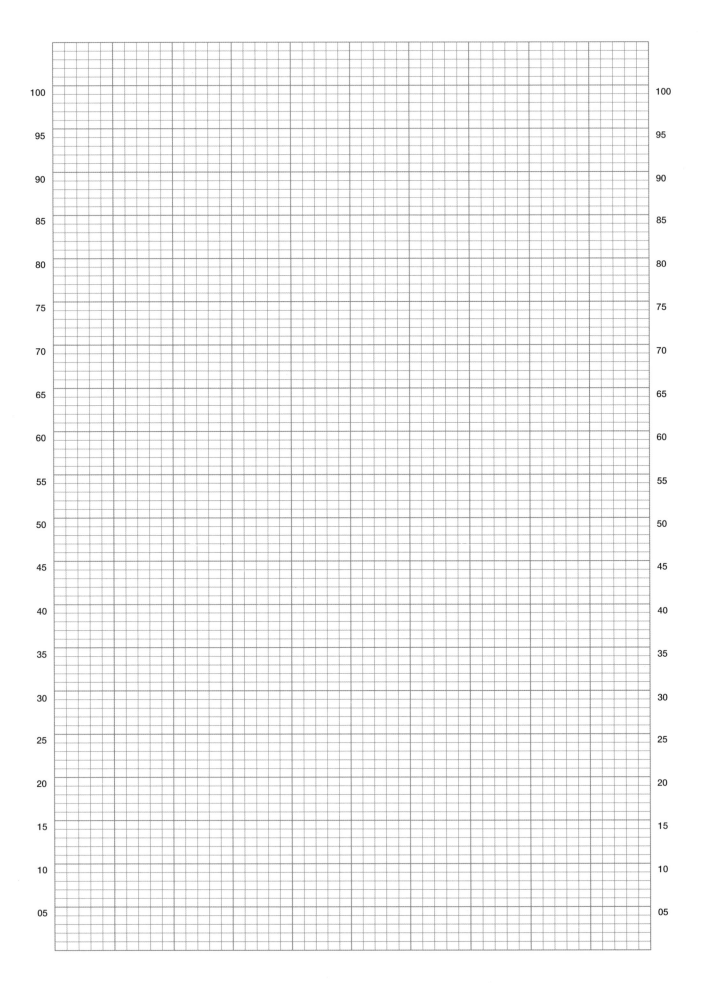

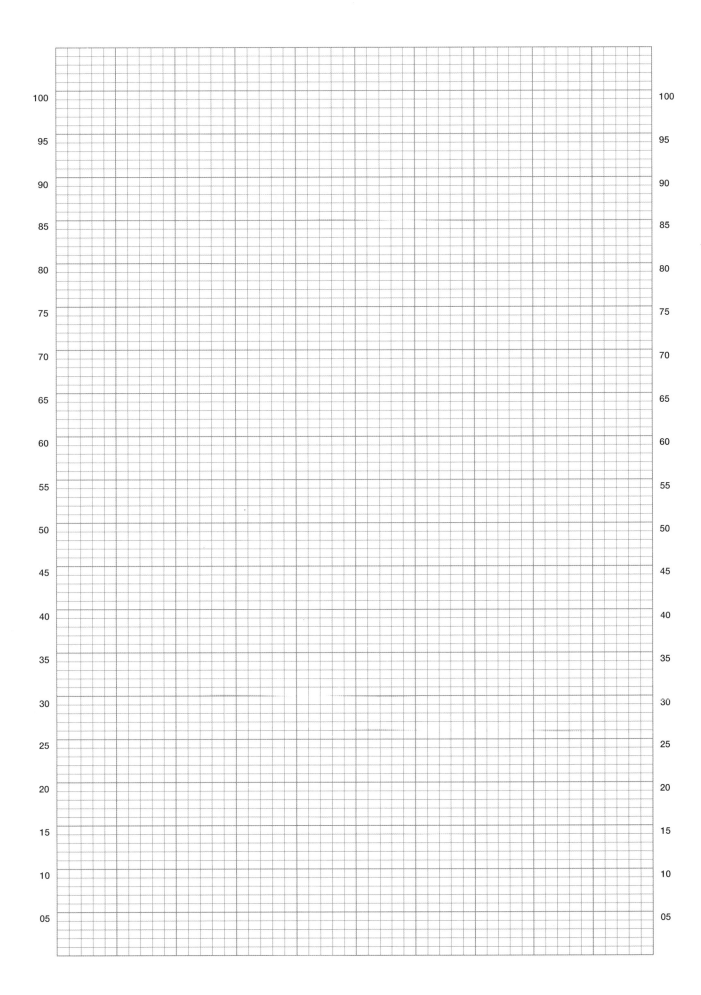

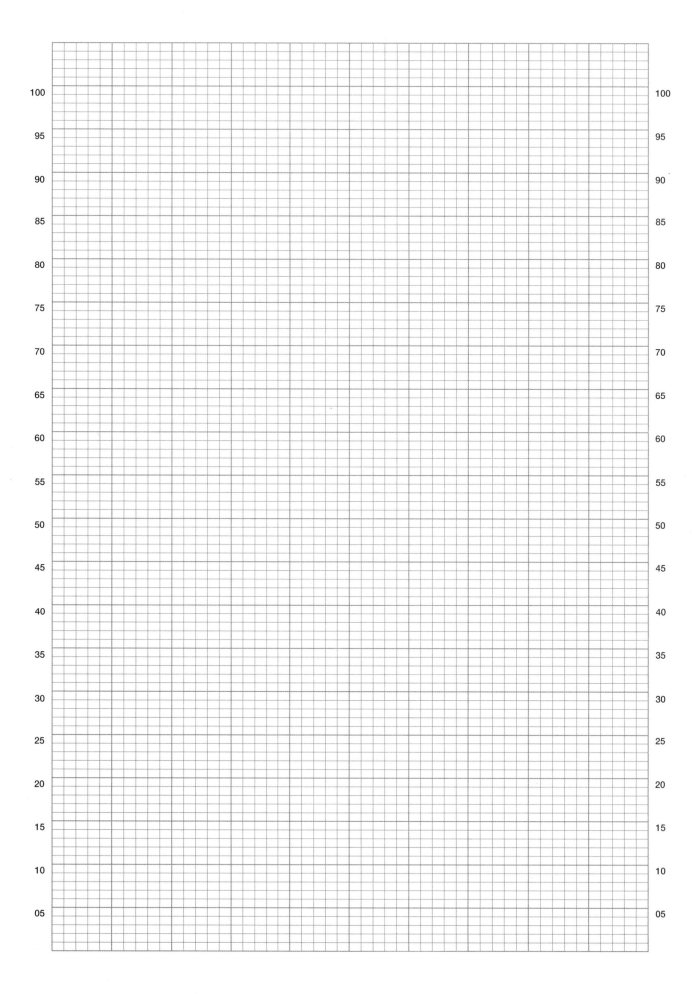

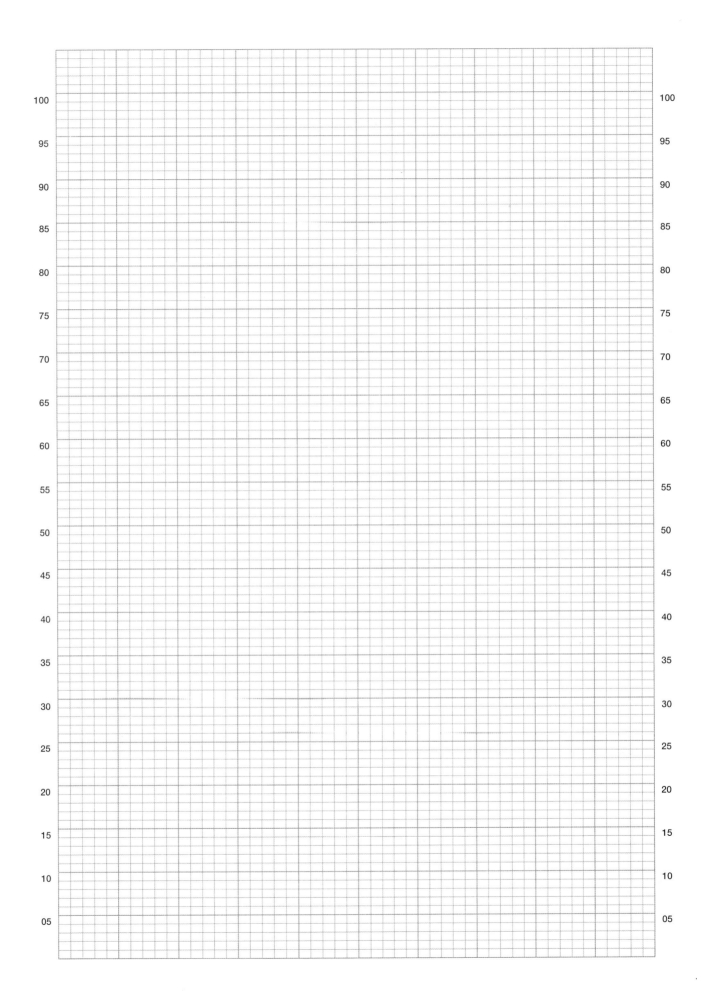

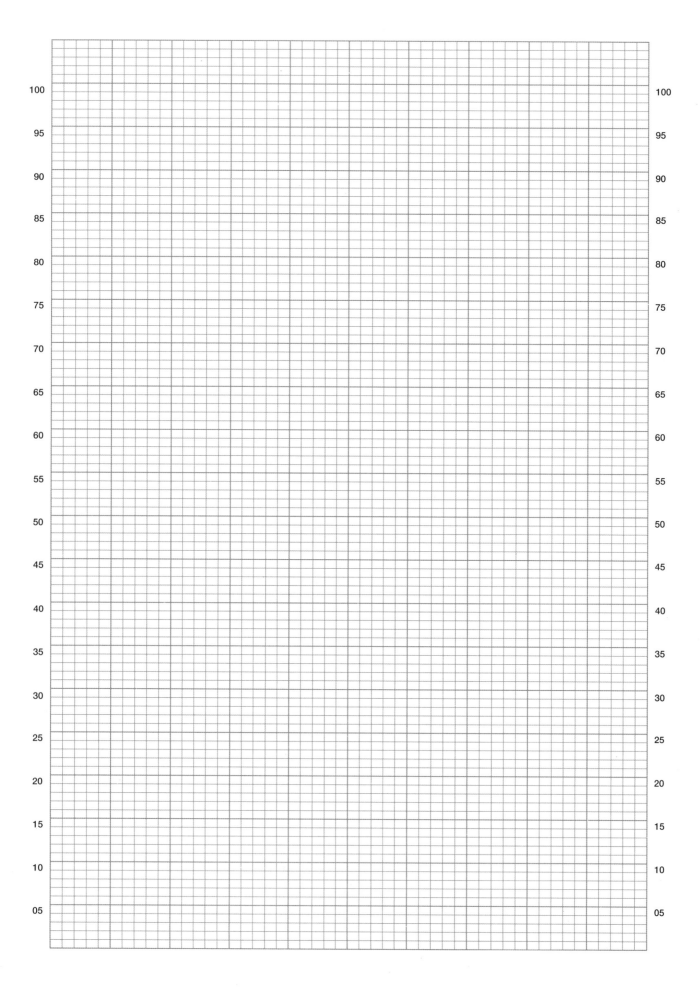

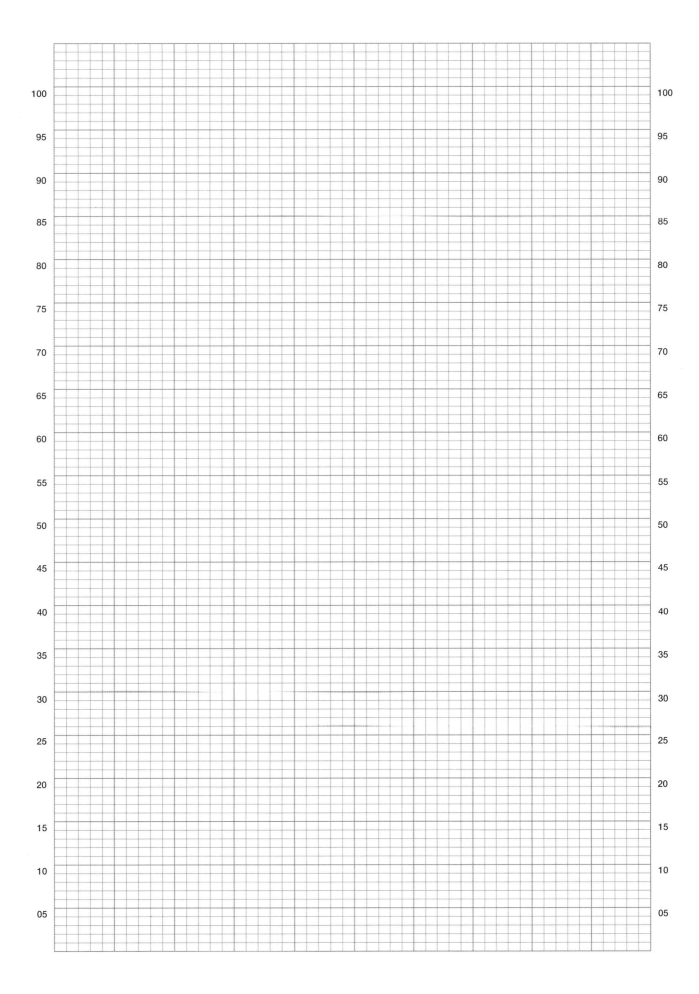

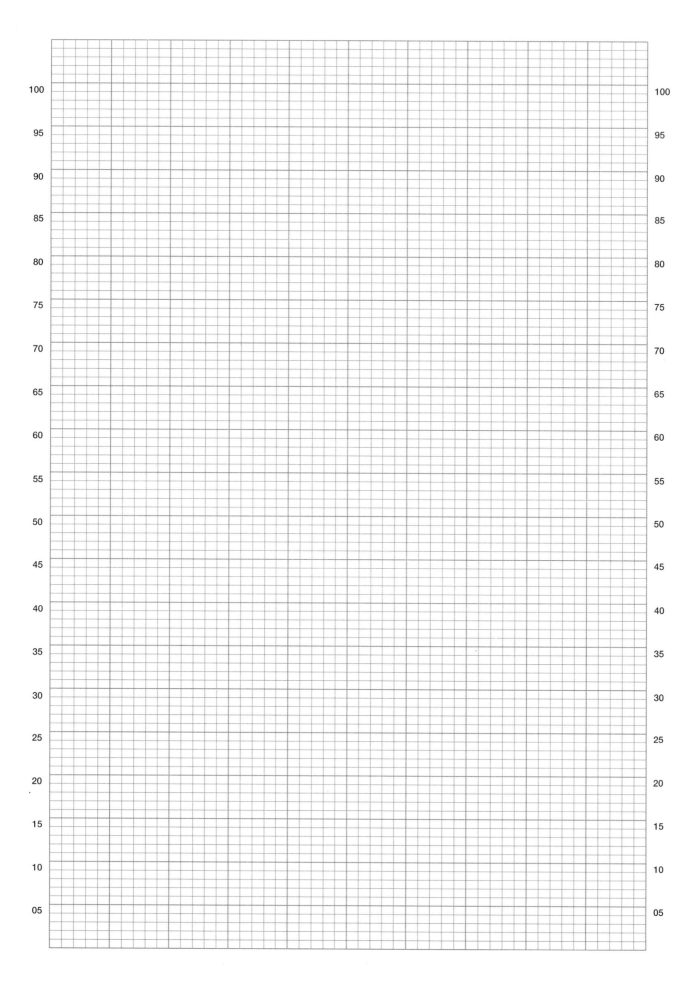

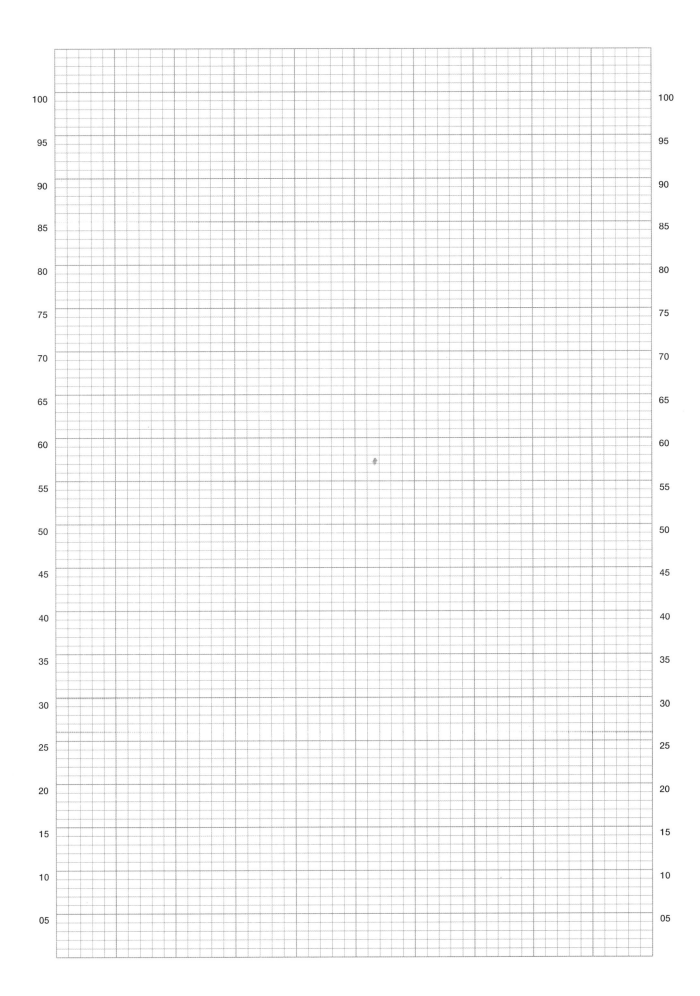

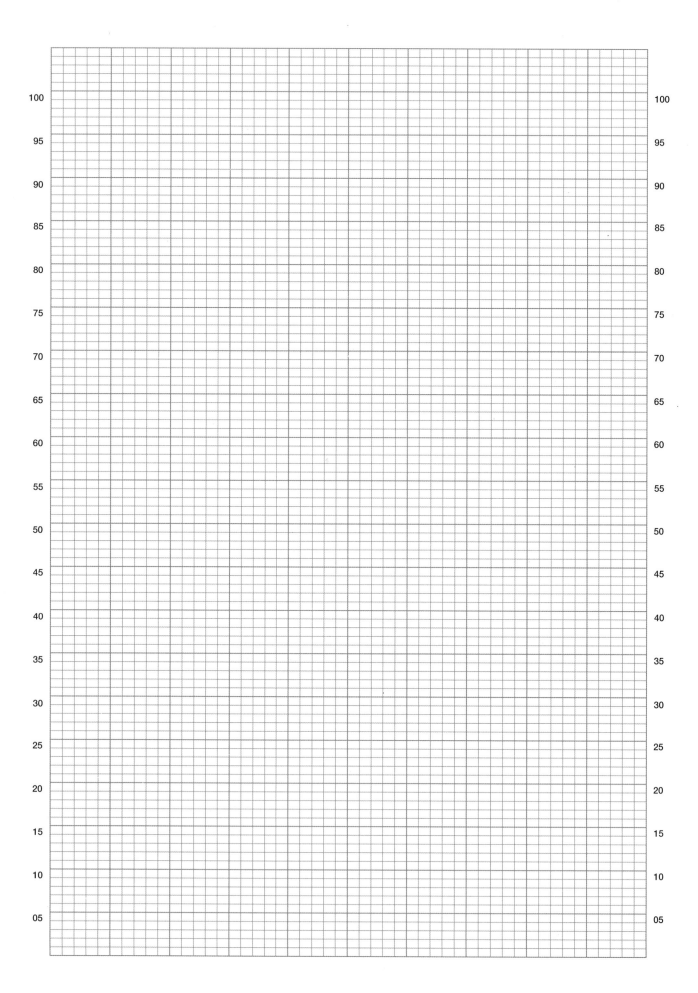

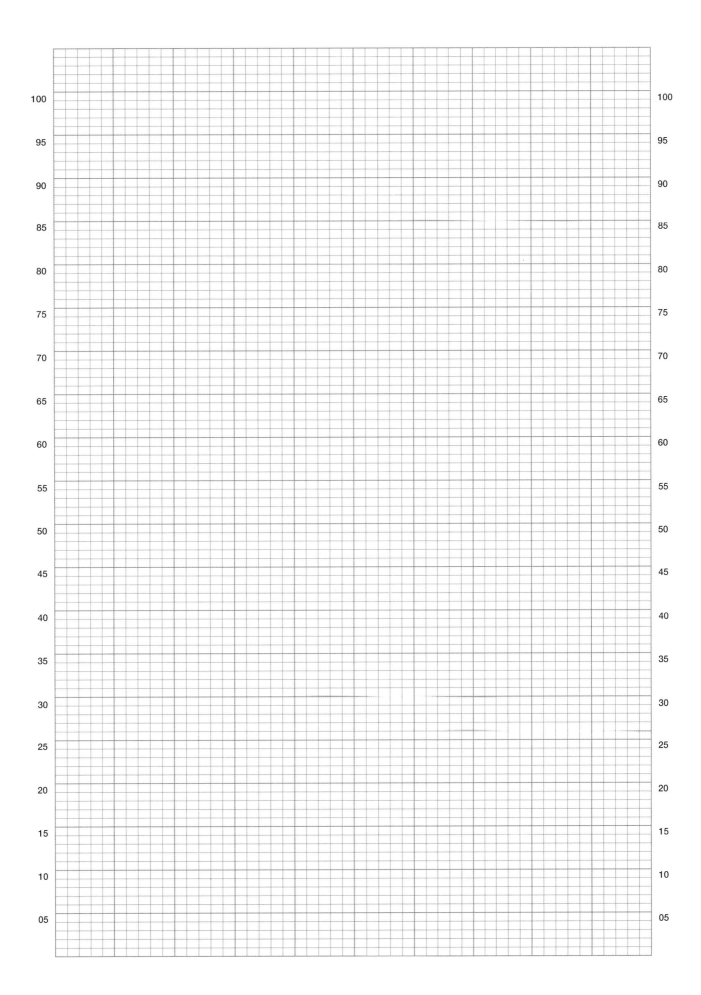

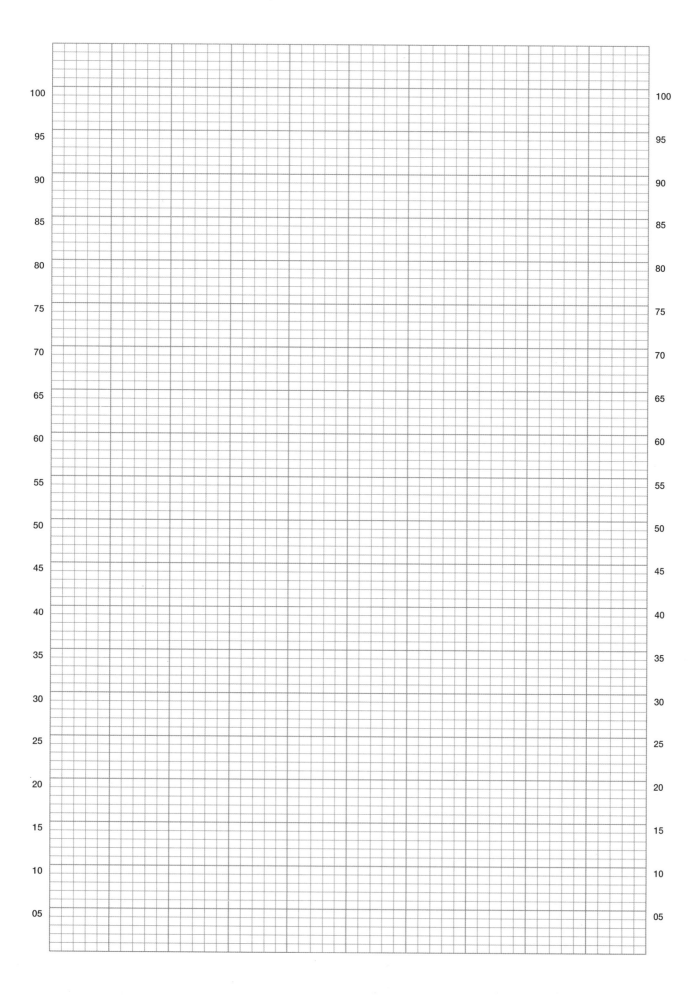

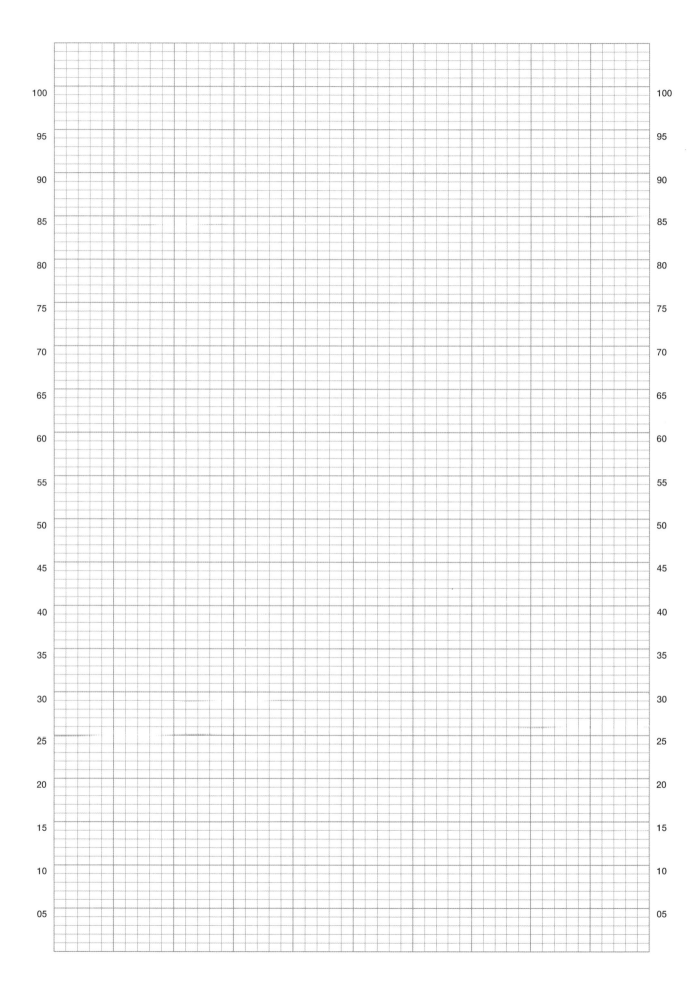

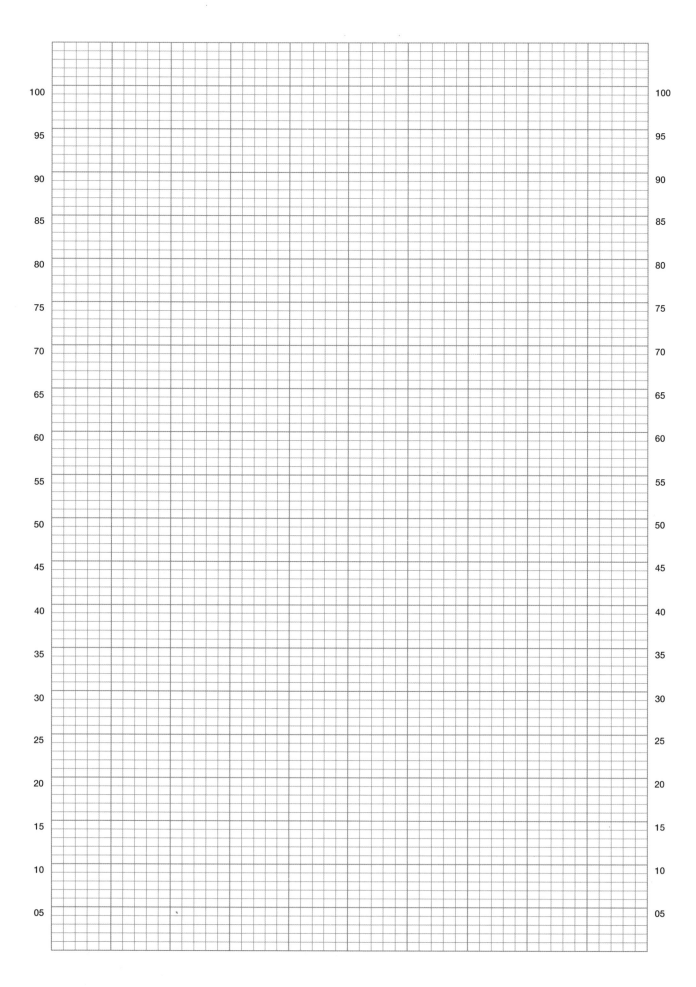

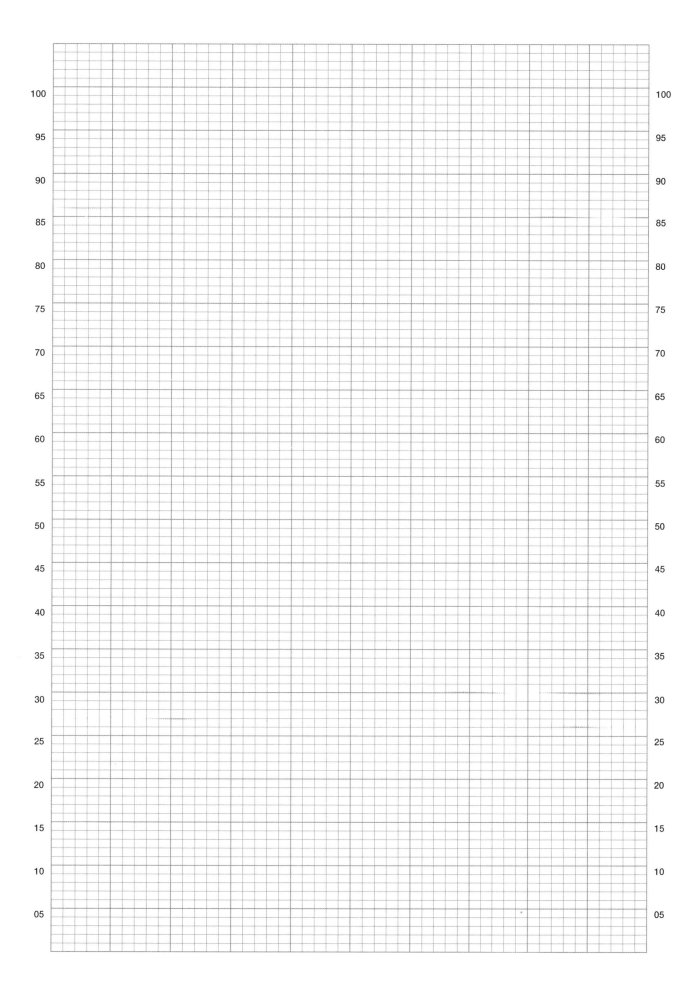

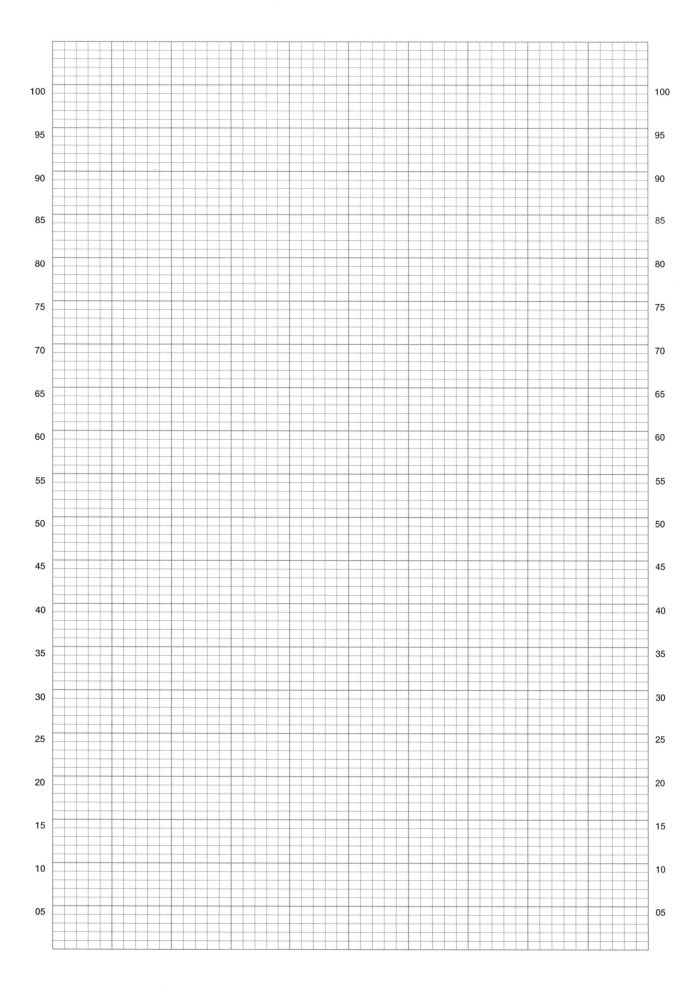

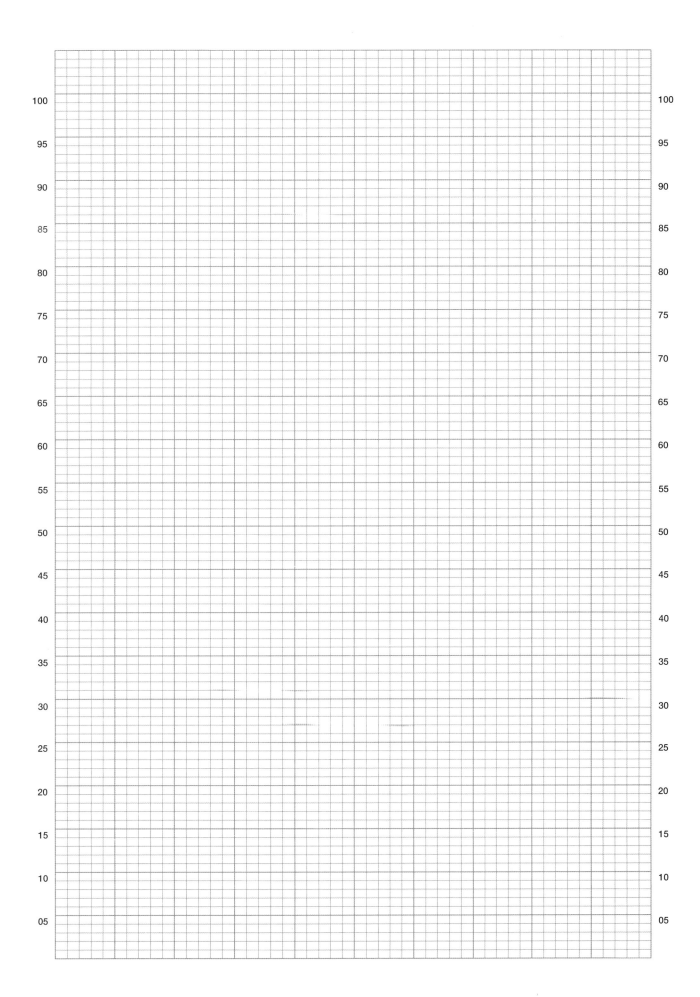

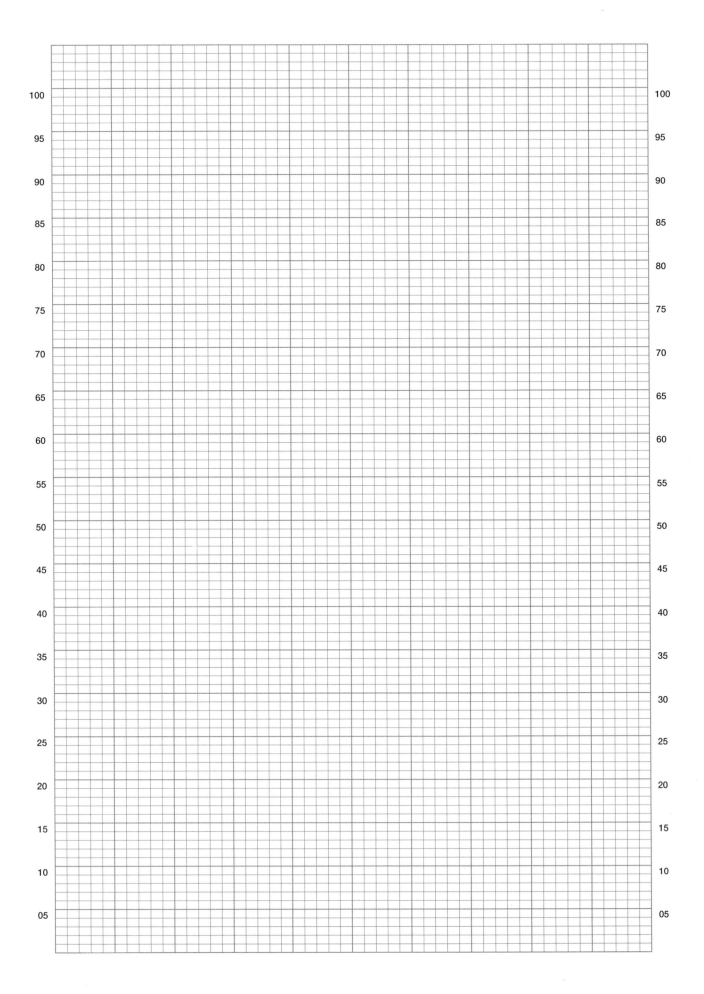

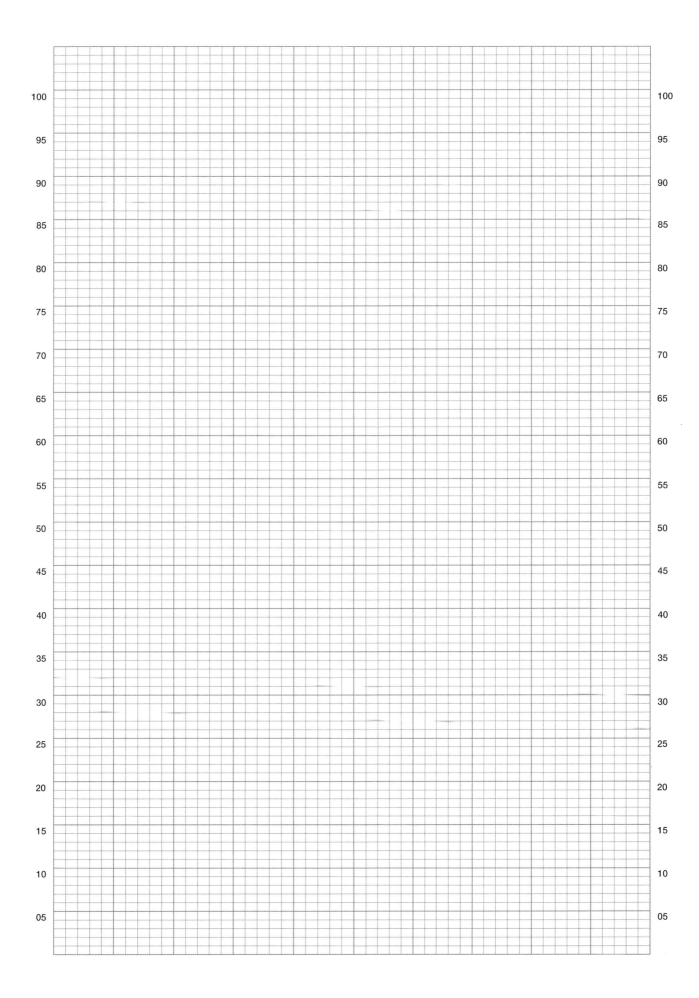

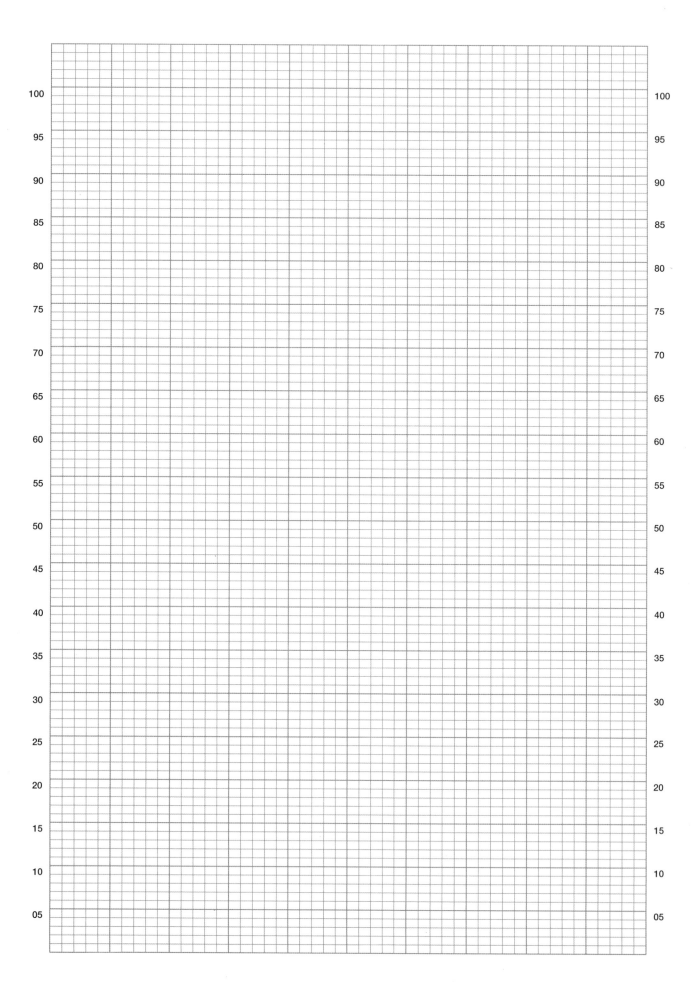

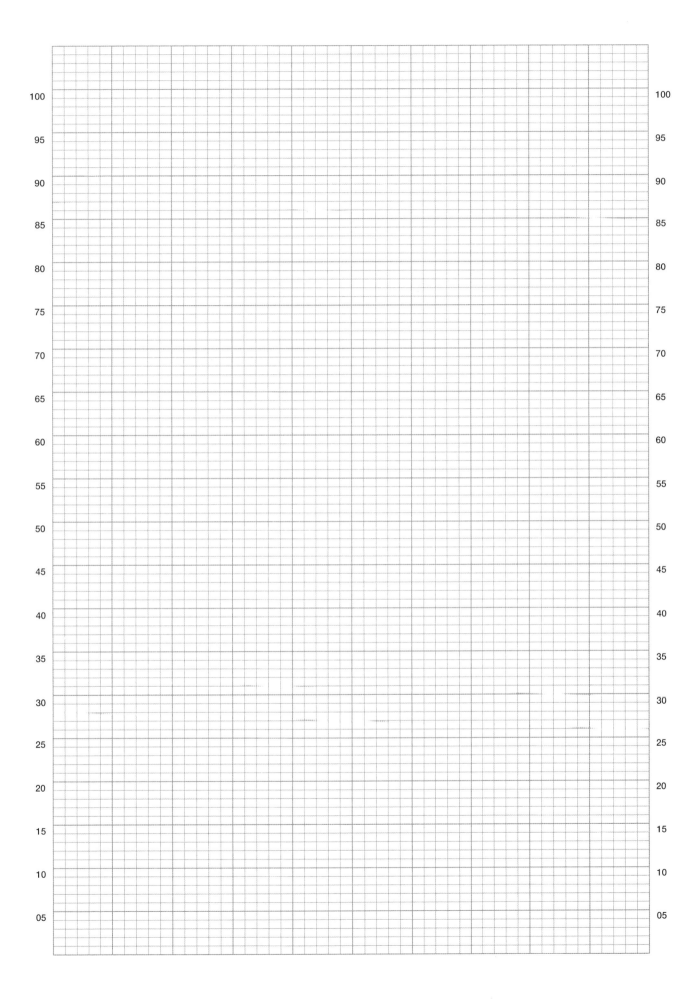

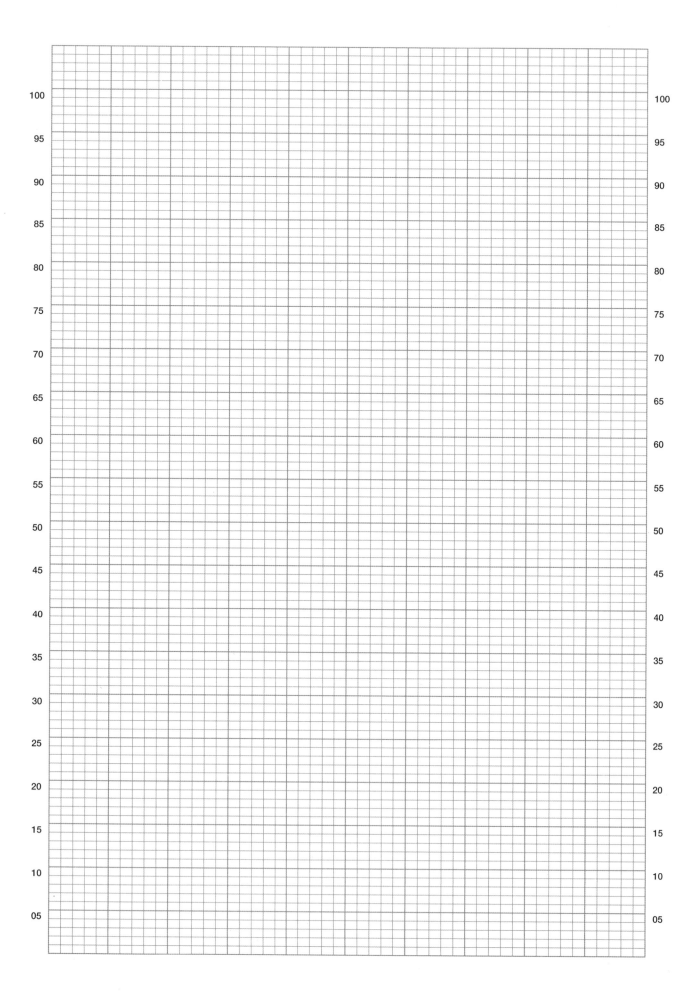

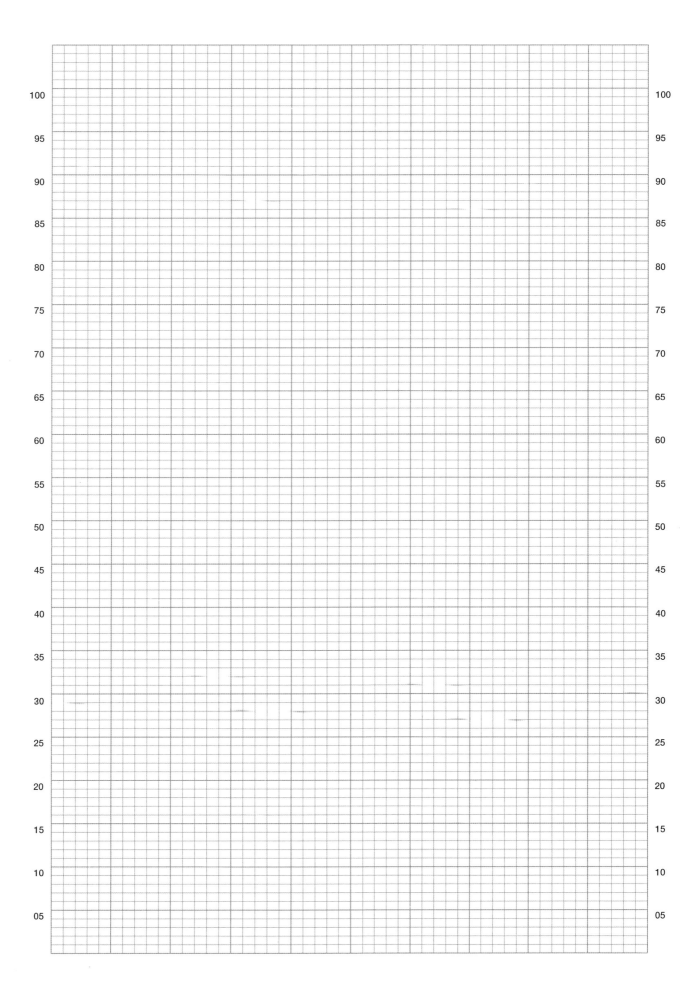

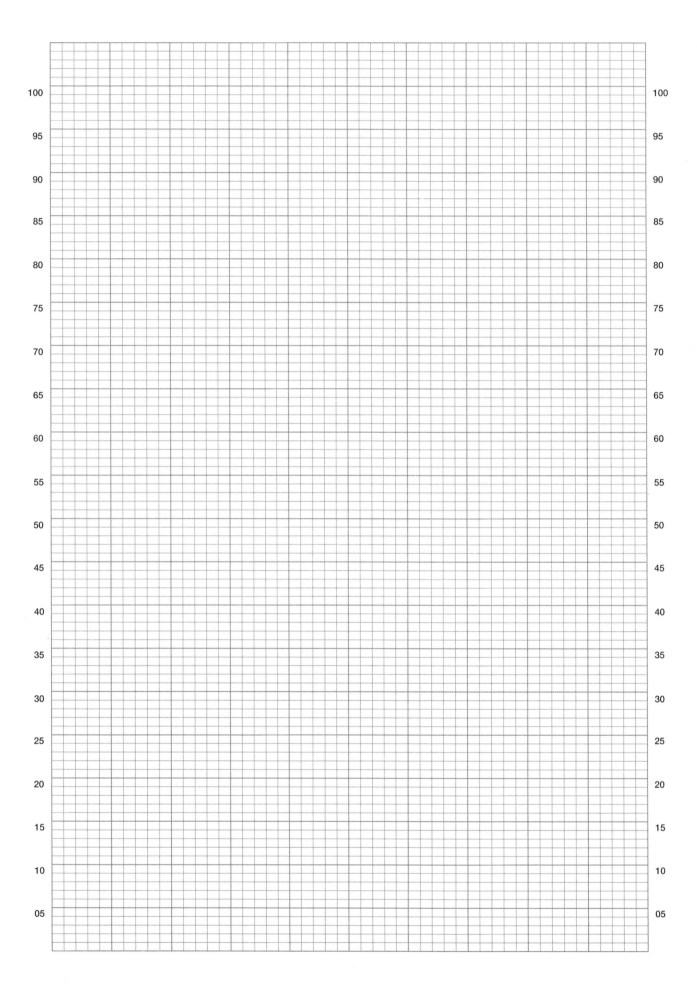

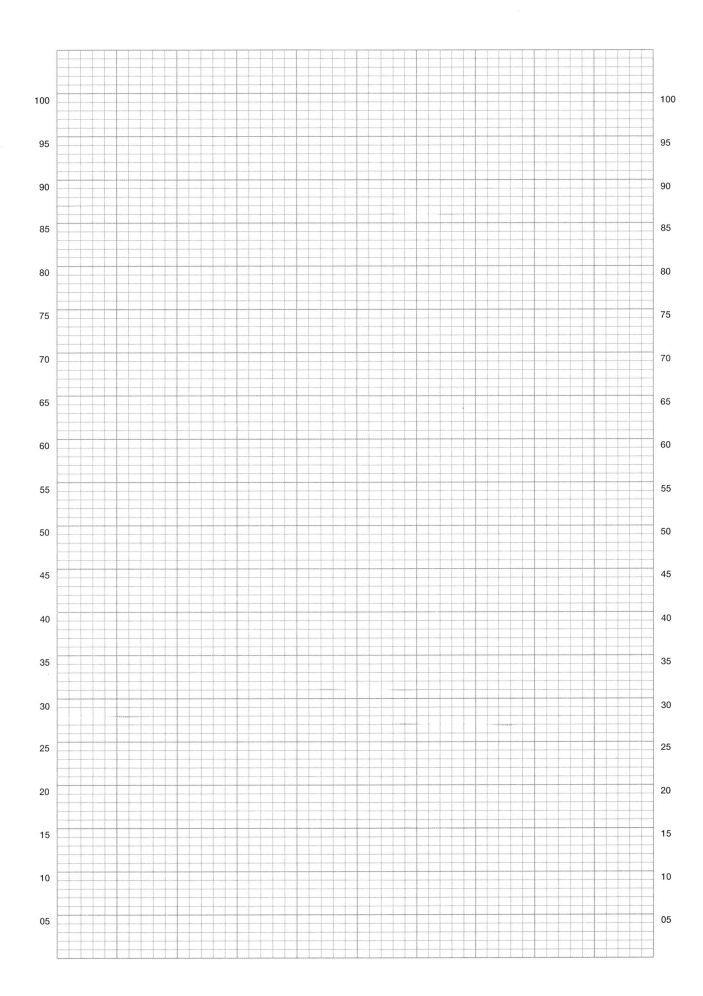

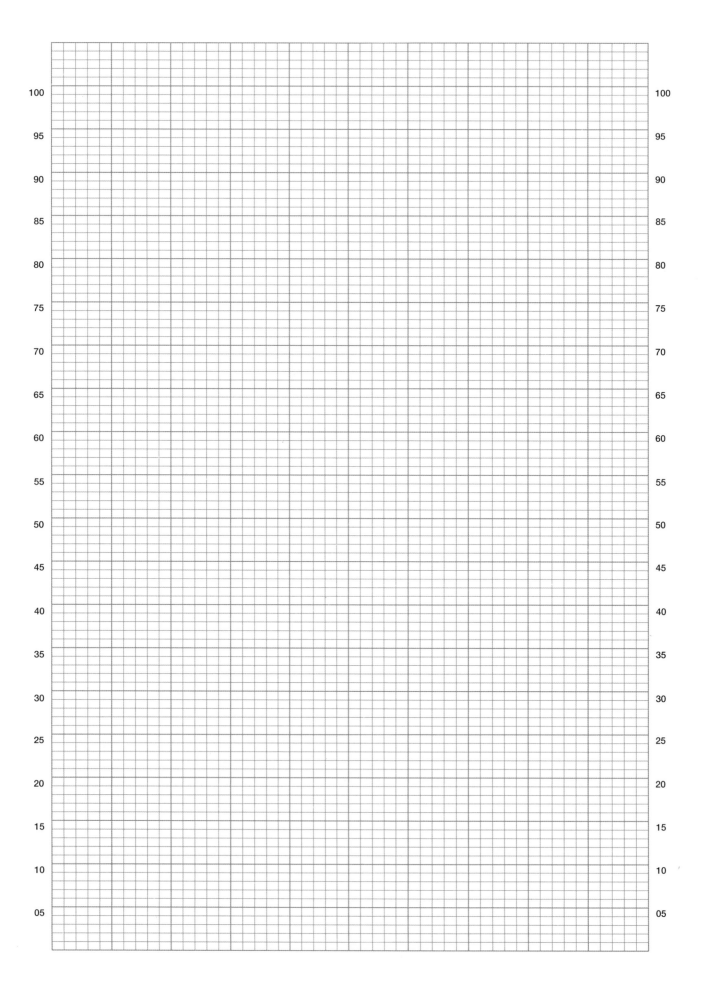

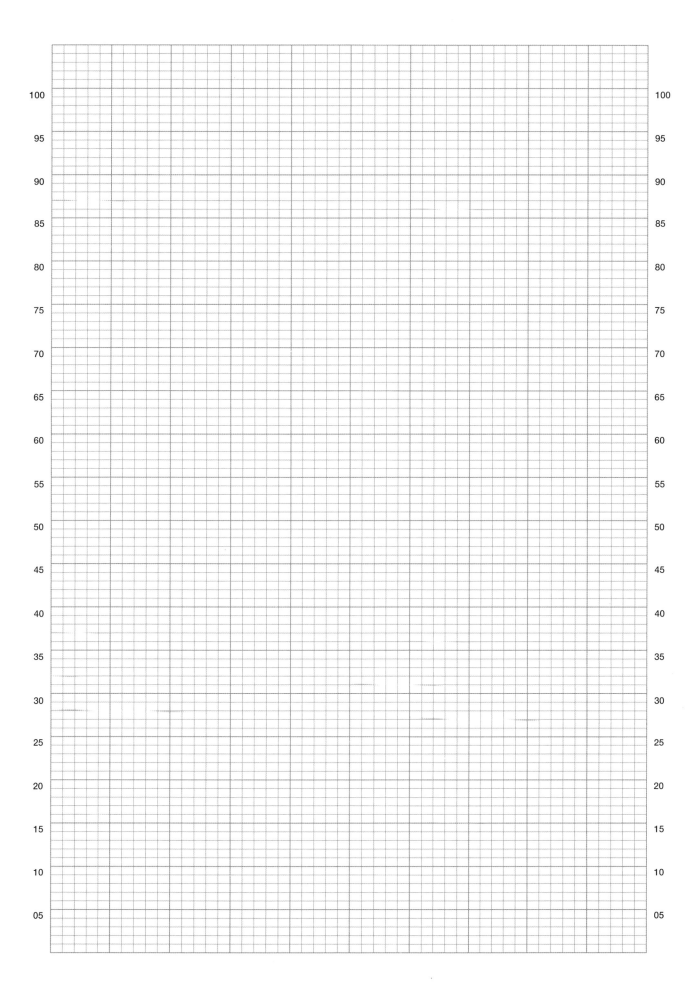

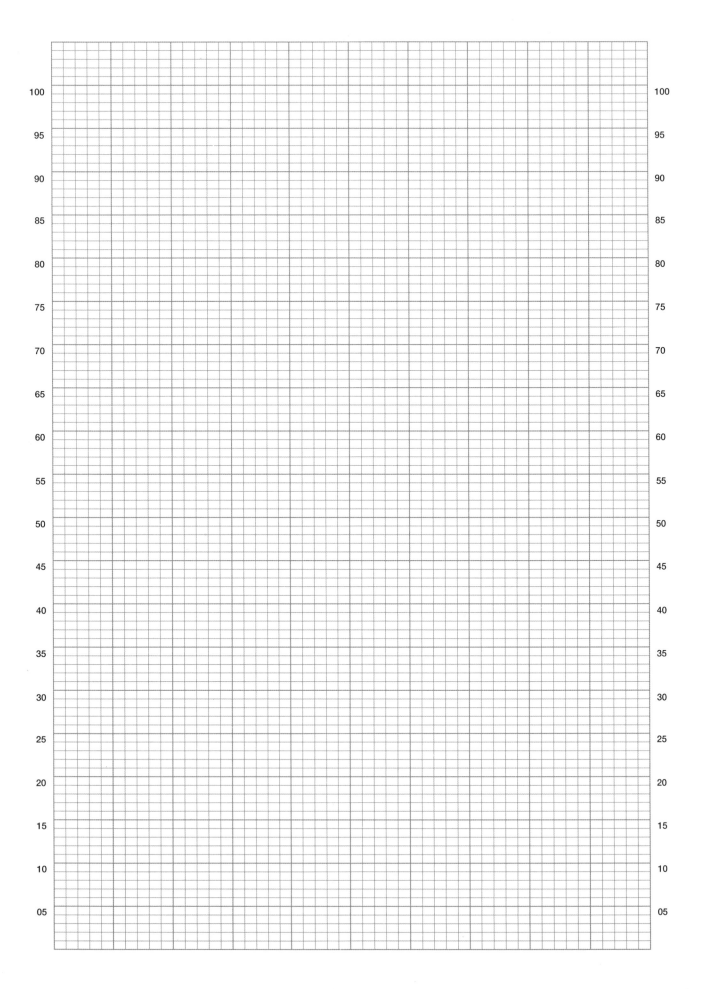

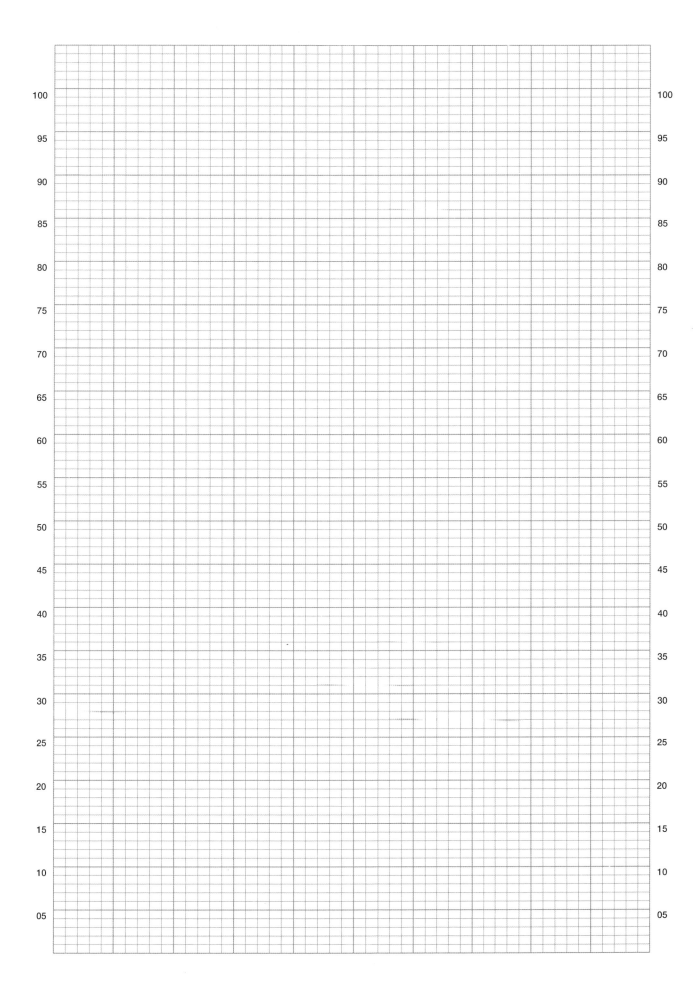

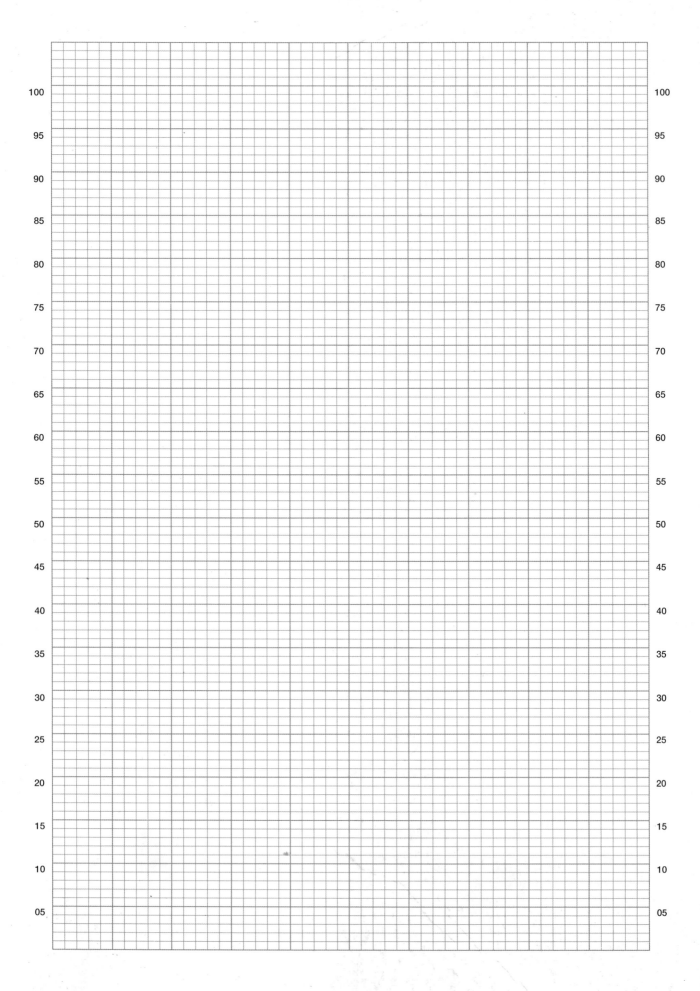